A Common Sense
EDUCATION
—— in ——
Uncommon Times
Caulbridge

DEBRA LAMBRECHT

Printed in the United States of America

First Printing, 2019
ISBN: 978-1-7339498-0-4

Library of Congress Control Number: 2019908783

Caulbridge, Inc. Publishing
1 St. Vincent Drive
San Rafael, CA 94903
www.caulbridgeschool.org

Dedication

To my daughter Rachel Rubinstein, the one person who continues to inspire and amaze me.

To the families of Caulbridge School who honor us with their children.

Contents

Introduction

When my daughter was in school, I felt like a more effective parent because of her teacher. Parents often count their blessings when they "get a good teacher"; or when they don't, they just struggle through the year as best they can. Throughout my career of training educators and consulting in schools, I have met many dedicated teachers and parents who question the old system and long for a more authentic education model – yet find themselves limited and ultimately compromised.

Every parent wants the best for their child. Maybe this desire comes naturally as an extension of your own happy childhood, or like me, you need to create a new possibility for a healthy family life. Believing this could be learned, I studied everything I could about child development and what children need – about education strategies, trends, and practices – in order to further my career in education and to better integrate my own journey. Once I became a parent, the real work began. I soon realized that when you have children, you come face to face with your Self. When you have a two-year-old, your own two-year-old issues come up; when she's eight, your eight-year-old issues surface; and when she turns fourteen, well... you have to be willing to keep going! Committed to my own growth, my ever-present mantra became, "Just keep me six months ahead of her."

Even though I felt effective as a parent, I was still holding out for the proof. Could I really break the cycle of dysfunction and abuse? Could I really enjoy a warm, nurturing family life? Only now that my daughter is grown, with a family of her own, am I convinced that my approach to parenting would work. And I eagerly look forward to the next wonderful phase: grandparenting.

Throughout my career I remained both a witness and a participant in the tumultuous world of education. With almost forty years as an educator, I saw the disconnect between healthy child development and academic goals of the schools. I developed programs to support students' social-emotional skills, and I watched how children who are nurtured become academically successful. Even the most effective new programs brought into schools to help children were ultimately rejected because schools were not ready for system-wide changes. After years of trying to influence the system, I came to realize that while it's not likely that we can change the system, we can break the cycle and operate with a new system that supports our children.

When a parent recently learned that I had started a school – and that I am writing a book, creating a new education model, and embarking on a journey to develop a network of Caulbridge Schools – he leaned back in his chair with a friendly, cocky grin, and said, "Well, that's a bit bold, don't you think?" I froze. What an enormous undertaking this is, and who am I to even attempt it? Yet, in an instant, I felt a warmth rise up and a certainty that only time and experience can provide.

Seeing the growing concern of children who are ill-equipped for learning intersect with the traditional education system which has become overwhelmed and unable to adapt, a bold response is indeed required. Caulbridge education began as a desire to step back, and to answer the more fundamental questions: "What is an ideal education for our time, for the children before us today? How can we break the cycle of dysfunction? Could we start with an intention to raise happy, healthy children?" Finding the answer to these questions within both, current research and collective wisdom, we opened our first school in Marin, California as part of a larger social mission to build a network of Caulbridge Schools.

At Caulbridge, we are courageous enough to teach in ways that authentically address child development, even when contemporary education practices run contrary. We are preparing children for a time of new paradigms, for jobs that have not yet been created, for unknown challenges and undiscovered solutions. In these unprecedented times of change and uncertainty, our world needs adaptive thinkers with strength of heart and character. It is in our striving to be better and our willingness to be open that we prepare for something we cannot yet imagine; that we become ready to meet the world and each other with open minds and hearts.

If you are a forward-thinking parent who wants more for your children – if you are a parent frustrated with the hit-or-miss of your child's educational experience – this book will come as a reassurance, a relief, and an answer for how to improve your child's entire learning experience. You'll find answers that might both surprise you and have you thinking, "Well, *that* makes sense!"

SECTION 1

Who's Failing Here? Our Children or The Schools?

Why Is My Child Struggling in School?

If your child has difficulties with recalling previous lessons, is easily distracted, or generally resists learning, there may be other factors at play. A child's academic struggles may be indications of other sensory-motor, social-emotional, or developmental challenges. Learning comes easily for children when they have a solid foundation of motor development, sensory processing, social confidence, and self-regulation or impulse control.

While these skills are essential for academic success, they are not necessarily developed through academics alone. The ability to process information and learn, for example, relies on spatial awareness, balance, and imagination. Children with under-developed sensory processing may appear scattered, have poor motor control, and are often drawn to sensory-seeking behaviors like fidgeting, pushing, or playing rough. When these foundational skills are under-developed, giving a child more hours of math lessons will not increase comprehension. What will increase comprehension is building proprioceptive capacity, also known as spatial awareness, in support of sensory and cognitive processing.

Paying attention to healthy motor development, sensory processing, and social skills will best prepare children for learning.

IN THE CLASSROOM

David, a fourth-grade student, was highly intelligent and savvy beyond his years. In his previous school, he had had social and behavior problems. Academically, his writing and math levels did not match his intellect. Upon enrolling him, his mother assured us that she'd get him a math tutor if needed, because she didn't want him to fall further behind. We suggested that we get to know him first before piling on more math, given that he was so resistant to the subject in the first place.

After just a few days, his teacher reported, "He doesn't know his right from his left!" You cannot hold a picture of place value if you don't know your right from your left. It is impossible to remember that you read from left to right and add from right to left. We worked for a couple of weeks with right/left games (crossing the mid-line), jumping rope (resisting gravity for vestibular system/balance), and climbing trees (core strength and spatial awareness). In a few weeks, we noticed new physical development in his body – and at about the same time, his math skills clicked in. He could now understand his math facts and quickly caught up to grade level.

50% of Children Will Not Be Able to Cope – How to Make Sure Yours Will

Fully half of our current population of children will be diagnosed with anxiety, depression, or a mood disorder by the time they are eighteen. While all children will experience stress and anxiety, half of them will not be able to cope! This is certainly an alarming trend; however, it can be shifted with the right educational environment.

Our young children are experiencing more stress and anxiety than any previous generation. According to the National Institute of Mental Health, teen suicide rates have increased by 30% for boys and 100% for girls in the past ten years, with anxiety and depression cited as the leading causes.

Why are our children so anxious? They live in an anxious world. The amount of information, technology, toxins, and trauma in our children's world can be a complete assault on the senses. Children are physical beings and learn everything through the senses. The increase in children's sensory-processing delays correlates both to their increased anxiety and their increasing inability to cope.

Sensory-processing and learning disorders are on the rise, with a recent study suggesting that one in five children experiences sensory challenges sufficient to disrupt their academic, social, and/or emotional development. Whether these challenges result from environmental influences or a child's particular circumstances, schools have become overwhelmed with special-needs students, which in recent years has led to the growth of a relatively new industry of educational therapists, sensory-integration specialists or occupational therapists offering services outside of school.

The STAR Institute for Sensory Processing Disorders defines the role of occupational therapy as "to work on the skills (occupations) people need to function in their daily lives. This often involves learning the skills necessary for play and schoolwork, and health relationships." Given the prevalence of sensory-processing concerns in our children, schools must respond to the developmental delays in children and the subsequent effects on learning and behavior.

IN THE CLASSROOM

Bryan came to Caulbridge with severe anxieties, particularly around school. In his previous pre-kindergarten, he had been demonstrating selective mutism and school refusal; not wanting to participate in activities because he put so much pressure on himself to be perfect. He often needed to be picked up early from school because of his fears and anxious behaviors.

During his "shadow day" (initial school visit), Bryan was calm and seemed to connect to his teachers and peers, though he made sure to announce upon arriving that he did not like math. When math time came, however, he was eager to "build" with the math manipulatives, and within a few days, he could encode and decode numbers 1-99.

Anxiety can put a child into fight-or-flight mode, and affect physical or sensory needs. Bryan was resistant to using the school restroom on his own – in fact, at his previous school, he often managed to last all day without using the bathroom. Given the privacy of a single-toilet restroom, and appropriate prompting from his teachers, Bryan felt safe and his physical needs were met.

The environment plays an important role for students with anxieties, and from his first day at Caulbridge, the new learning for Bryan was now focused on how to raise his hand – and to listen to others speaking – because he had so much to say!

This is the first generation of children who are growing up able to push a button here, and something happens over there! We are witnessing the effects of this phenomenon in the increased desire for immediate gratification, decreased tolerance for complex relationships, and a reliance on technology for answers.

Problem solving, logic, and higher-level thinking all rely on the ability to understand process, as well as how components fit together. Children want to know how things work, even before they can cognitively understand it all. For the young child, the ability to understand process happens by experiencing it first-hand.

In the past, family and cultural norms were passed down to children from adults and elders. With the rising impact of social media and advanced technologies, peers are increasingly more influential than adult family members. Peers are the influencers and arbitrators of cultural norms. Culture and expectations are being passed across, peer to peer, rather than passed down from adult to child. While peers may be the best source of contemporary information and trends, peers may lack the emotional and relationship skills, life experiences, and maturity needed to develop a child's sense of self. Children's creativity, independence, maturation, and confidence are rooted in the context of solid relationships with nurturing adults.

Only when children establish a foundation of dependence and compliance with trusting adults can they begin to develop independence and creativity. This dependence and compliance, or attachment relationship, works to establish trust and safety. Once a child experiences the world as a safe place, they will be able to fully develop their own integrity, ethical thinking, initiative, compassion, critical-thinking skills, and self-confidence to navigate their world.

The need for a trusting attachment relationship extends into the school years for children. Schools must be unwavering in the task of providing an emotionally safe environment for children.

The Cost of a Missed Childhood

In writing this chapter, I reached out to Derek Rubinstein, Psy.D. who has a thriving psychotherapy practice in San Francisco and San Rafael, working with adults, children, and families. We are fortunate to have Dr. Rubinstein serve as our school psychologist, teaching mindfulness to our students and participating on our faculty. While we generally focus on the school setting and how our school environment can positively impact child development, I asked Derek to reflect on his therapy practice – and speak from a clinical perspective – which extends beyond the classroom. Here are a few of the questions and responses from our conversation.

What happens when childhood needs are not met? What is the cost emotionally, socially, etc.?

Children have unique developmental needs, and when they don't get met, there are predictable, negative consequences that can have long-lasting impact. In my clinical practice, the most common underlying issue in children is dysregulation – when a child has difficulty managing and regulating their body, behaviors, emotions, and/or attention.

Common signs of a child who is dysregulated:

- Frequent tantrums and meltdowns
- Difficulty focusing attention and learning
- Chronic anxiety
- Aggressive behavior

- Impulsivity
- Psychological and behavioral rigidity
- Social-emotional difficulties

As these challenges persist, children begin to develop negatively distorted perceptions of themselves and others. Over time, this can result in secondary problems such as low self-esteem and disrupted interpersonal connections with both peers and adults. This can become a vicious self-perpetuating and reinforcing cycle, especially when early interventions are missed.

When a child's basic needs are consistently left unmet, children come to feel that something is wrong with their needs, feel a lack of safety, and to various degrees develop mental-health issues, difficulties learning, and even physiological collapse as the nervous system of children depends on adults to stay regulated.

How do we attempt to compensate for those unmet needs as adults, and why is that adult effort so futile?

Even in the face of unspeakable traumas, children can be incredibly resilient. However, when basic needs are not satisfied, the nervous system becomes increasingly dysregulated and children come to rely more heavily on suboptimal or maladaptive coping strategies in attempts to compensate for emotional, psychological, interpersonal, and neurophysiological deficits. As these children grow up and transition into adulthood, they develop predictable psychological and physiological symptoms such as chronic anxiety, depression, low self-esteem, interpersonal difficulties, somatic complaints, and even addiction.

It is critical to develop these self-regulatory capacities and skills during the developmental years as the brain is growing, the neural circuitry that connects and integrates the different regions of the brain are forming, and the mind is developing mental models of how one views oneself, others, and the world around them. While modern brain science and psychotherapy research show us that adults can change their brain and behavior, that effort requires deliberate and long-term behavioral and psychotherapeutic work to undo old neuronal and psychological patterning – and re-learn more adaptive ways of being, acting, and relating.

Fostering healthy development during the formative years – through nurturing relationships, supportive environments, and focusing on prevention efforts as needed – is clearly the preferable and more commonsense approach. Of course, many children need more specific or targeted interventions, and when these are provided in a timely manner, the harmful effects of unmet needs are diverted and long-term outcomes are greatly improved.

Is there hope for ensuring that these needs are met in our children?

Our capacity for connection, with both ourselves and others, is a defining feature of emotional and psychological health. Attachment theory states that a loving, attuned, and responsive emotional and physical connection to at least one primary caregiver is critical to successful childhood development. A secure attachment with our caregivers lays the foundation for healthy physical, emotional, and cognitive development. At birth and into the early years, a baby is entirely dependent on their caregivers for survival, and to regulate their internal and external states. Over time, the caregiver's co-regulation of their child's states through warm and responsive interactions teach children how to understand, express, and modulate their thoughts, feelings, behaviors, and needs.

Through this co-regulation process, children become increasingly capable of managing their feelings and getting their needs met on their own, and become secure in their dependence as well as their independence. Children learn to feel safe, trusting of the world around them, and connected to their body and their emotions. These are important developmental experiences, as they enable children to leave the secure base of their caregivers and home to explore and interact with the world around them. With a secure attachment, children grow up feeling a sense of self-regulation, well-being, and the capacity for healthy connection. As children make their way toward adulthood, this internal architecture provides the foundation for learning, growing, and successfully navigating the inevitable triumphs and challenges of life with a sense of meaning, purpose, aliveness, and self-efficacy.

How do you see the environment and teaching at Caulbridge working to specifically meet the developmental needs of children?

While caregivers lay the foundation for a secure attachment, children spend significant time throughout their developmental years in school, interacting with their teachers and peers. Teachers form meaningful relationship to their students, and they can further reinforce secure attachments – and positively influence children – in developing social, emotional, and academic success. Caulbridge educators work from a child-development perspective and understand that meeting the child's needs relevant to their phase of development is foundational to learning and school success.

The school environment provides the holding container, and it is a significant factor in setting the stage for optimal development. The Caulbridge classrooms are calm and inviting. Time in nature is a critical component of regulating a child's nervous system, aiding their ability to regulate their bodies, emotions, and behaviors. Teaching through the senses can help anchor new skills and knowledge with practical experiences. Clear expectations and boundaries held by nurturing adults will help to shift a child's habits and behaviors that may not serve them.

"The research is really clear on this point. Kids who achieve the best outcomes in life – emotionally, interpersonally, and even educationally – have parents who raise them with a high degree of connection and nurturing, while also communicating and maintaining clear limits and high expectations. Their parents remain consistent, while still interacting with them in a way that communicates love, respect, and compassion. As a result, the kids are happier, do better in school, get into less trouble, and enjoy more meaningful relationships.

Connection means that we give our children our attention, that we model respectful and loving relationship, that we listen, that we value their efforts and contributions, and that we communicate – verbally and non-verbally – that we are on their side and understand their needs." Daniel Siegel is a clinical professor of psychiatry at the UCLA School of Medicine, the founding co-director of the Mindful Awareness Research Center, and the author of several books on child development and neuroscience. While Dr. Siegel refers to the parent relationship here, children spend a large part of their day with teachers, who have significant influence in this healthy child development.

Common Practice vs. Common Sense

Many schools have similar goals for their students: fostering creativity, academic success, social-emotional skills, and positive classroom behavior. While these are common-sense goals, the common practice in schools often runs counter to achieving these goals.

Creativity: Walk into most classrooms, and you'll see academic posters and student projects displayed on every inch of the available wall space – and even hanging from the ceiling. The goal is to stimulate student creativity. It may seem logical that exposing children to as many different experiences as possible would foster curiosity and creativity; however, it can actually have the opposite effect. Overexposure risks overloading and destabilizing children. Instead, we must pay attention to fostering healthy integration of experiences with the senses, using body movement, exposure to nature, and respectful social interaction. When children develop a foundation of trusting themselves and their world, creativity, curiosity, and learning naturally unfold.

Academics: Based on the belief that all children learn differently, teachers will often teach math in several different ways, hoping that students will find the way that works for them. This common practice may only confuse children, and it does not support strong academics and coherent learning. While it's true that children process information differently, we know there are specific elements to effective learning, that when in place, all children can learn. Children are naturally inquisitive; their brains and bodies develop naturally toward new capacities and new learning. With rare exception, a student's academic deficits are symptoms of underlying developmental delays, anxieties, sensory-motor or sensory-processing delays. Common sense tells us that when a child is struggling with academics, something is in the way. These struggles are a red flag, and they become an obvious point of assessment or exploration. Explicit teaching of structured academics in a nurturing environment will support learning for all children.

Friendships: School is the most natural environment to make new friends, including some that will last a lifetime. Some children are more socially adept, while some have fewer social abilities. The common practice in traditional schools is to let students naturally find their friends and social groups. Since social-emotional skills are such a strong component of healthy child development and learning, it is important to support a child's social development. Assuming that children who isolate themselves from others are shy, and just need to make new friends, is to ignore the sometimes-paralyzing anxieties of peer social interactions. Assuming that aggressive behaviors are the outward signs of a bully is to miss possible emotional insecurities, or likely delayed sensory development. These assumptions may lead to artificial social situations, or to punishing a child for their own anxiety or sensory delays. A more effective solution is to help foster spatial awareness and balance, which will contribute to a child's ability to relate to their environment – and ultimately, make friends.

Focus: An essential skill, focus can be taught. An unintended consequence of children growing up in a faster, technology- and media-centered, digitally connected, more-new-now world is that they have difficulty with focus and have shorter attention spans than children in the past. As these "digital natives" show up to school with a decreased ability to focus, teachers often try anything they can to capture the attention of their students, using fast-moving activities and flashy lessons. Unfortunately, this common practice only exacerbates the issue.

Since the ability to focus is essential to all learning, a more helpful strategy is to help students master the ability to direct their attention. Preparing the body for learning is much like an athlete warming up before any physical undertaking. These warm-up activities bring more blood and oxygen flow to the brain, focusing energy into the task at hand. Only when the muscles, organs, and brain are alert, and working in sync with each other, is the body ready for learning.

Participation in Class: In a typical classroom, teachers spend much of their lesson time managing classroom behavior, often trying to redirect a student's attention to the lesson at hand. When that doesn't work, new consequences are added on as the child's behavior often escalates.

We must never assume a child who is acting out, not paying attention, and refusing to participate is simply trying to get away with something or just can't keep up academically. These assumptions will lead to a child's being ignored or punished, and eventually sent to remediation services as he falls behind the class. Instead, Caulbridge begins with the assumption that the child's behavior is taking care of something. With this perspective, we work to create an inclusive, nurturing environment where children's needs are met.

Children Who Fidget

"Children fidgeting is an indication that they need to move!" says Pediatric Occupational Therapist and educator Angela Hanscom. Her popular blog post "Why children fidget – And what we can do about it" explains her findings: "We quickly learned, after further testing, that most of the children in the classroom had poor core strength and balance. In fact, we tested a few other classrooms and found that when compared to children from the early 1980s, only one out of twelve children had normal strength and balance. Only one! Oh my goodness, I thought to myself. These children need to move!"

"Ironically," Ms. Hanscom continues, "many children are walking around with an underdeveloped vestibular (balance) system today – due to restricted movement. Children are going to class with bodies that are less prepared to learn than ever before. With sensory systems not quite working right, they are asked to sit and pay attention. Children naturally start fidgeting in order to get the movement that their body so desperately needs, yet that small fidgeting is not enough movement to turn their brain on. What happens when the children start fidgeting? We ask them to sit still and pay attention; therefore, their brain goes back to sleep."

IN THE CLASSROOM

Children often arrive at school after a hurried morning at home, maybe waking up late, searching for their shoes or favorite hat. In the car, they may be eating, arguing with siblings, listening to music, or hearing the news. Once at school, they are excited to see their friends and perhaps a bit anxious about the day. Students at Caulbridge begin each day with "morning circle" activities that will include beanbag toss, balancing and jumping, or other ways to move the body and focus the mind in preparation for learning. Movement and speech activities in the circle time also work to bring the students together as a cohesive group.

When it Comes to Learning, the Mind Follows the Body

When adrenaline builds up due to anxiety or sensitivities, the body goes into hyper-alert and the mind shuts down. A rush of adrenaline might help us cross the finish line or warn us of danger, yet that same adrenaline can get trapped in the body, bringing increased levels of the stress hormone cortisol. In addition to the familiar tantrums, meltdowns, or social-emotional challenges, this accumulated stress hormone may also be evidenced by your child's disrupted sleeping, eating, or learning habits.

When a child is in the midst of a tantrum, it becomes impossible for them to hear you. Only when the body becomes calm or re-regulated can that behavior shift.

Children can get locked into rigid behaviors and habits where it becomes impossible to take in new information. Developing a child's ability to learn, as well as shifting behaviors toward a growth mindset, requires warm-up activities, both physically and emotionally.

Developing neural pathways and creating optimal brain function are essential foundations for learning. Caulbridge employs regular classroom activities to support basic hand-eye coordination, sensory-motor skills, body awareness, reflexes, focused attention, coordination, spatial perception, and ocular motor control. Using developmental movement, nature, and human interaction, we both challenge and orient the senses.

IN THE CLASSROOM

In his previous school, Ethan couldn't handle the chaos and constant transitions of his class. He would refuse to move from one activity to the next – and when pushed, he could begin kicking and hitting. He did not demonstrate these behaviors at home, only at school, so his mother kept him home for several weeks looking for a more nurturing school environment for her son.

As Ethan was getting to know the routines at Caulbridge, as well as his peers and teachers, there were times where transitions from one class time to another caused him to freeze, refusing to move with the group. Knowing that when he dropped into this "freeze, fight, or flight" mode, his reasoning skills were shut off, his teacher would stay near to him, while also giving him enough space to feel safe. She used only a few words, and found a sensory experience that helped bring his attention back into his body. As a result of holding strong boundaries and redirecting Ethan's awareness back into his body, these periods of refusal soon decreased from daily to weekly – and now they happen only rarely and can be quickly re-focused.

IN THE CLASSROOM

First-grader Justin had an older brother at home who exposed him to violent media images. In class, Justin would often become distracted by what he called "the movie playing in my head." At times, the images Justin was recalling were so overwhelming that he would hit himself in the head, "trying to get them out."

Often lost in his own overly stimulated imagination, Justin was distracted during class times, causing him to miss the lessons. His teacher watched for his physical cues, and developed a strategy with Justin's approval that when she saw him disengage from reality, she would place her hand on his shoulder, which signaled to him to tap his foot three times. This simple sensory experience quickly re-engaged Justin in his work and the lesson.

Sensory Processing and Learning Disorders

Sensory experiences fuel the brain, building healthy neural pathways for optimal brain development. Sensory Integration is "the ability to register and process the type, quantity, and intensity of sensation provided by the environment, resulting in behaviors and feeling states that are either organized or disorganized." (STAR Institute for Sensory Processing Disorders).

Sensory-Processing Disorder is not a disease, but rather a condition that is assessed using a set of symptoms, characteristics, or behaviors. There is a wide range of this condition, from sensory-processing delays or differences to sensory-processing disorders, which is when the symptoms interfere with a person's functioning.

Typical symptoms might include:

* Oversensitive or over-reacts to touch, noise, or smells.
* Unaware of being bumped or unaware they have bumped into someone.
* Constant motion.
* Sudden mood changes, tantrums, or outbursts.
* Easily distracted; difficulty focusing.
* Confuses similar-sounding words; speech lacks fluency; rhythm is hesitant.
* Difficulty reading.
* Difficulty transitioning; gets stuck in a task.

- Craves physical, rough play or wrestling.

- Difficulty learning new motor tasks and prefers sedentary activities.

Most challenging behaviors can be shifted by addressing these symptoms of underlying sensory processing delays. When the brain/body connection is strengthened, new skills and capacities can emerge.

Rarely are sensory integration delays related exclusively to one sensory function. A diagnosis can include dyspraxia, over-responsiveness or under-responsiveness, as well as the ability to discriminate or recognize a distinction – for each of the senses!

Sensory-processing diagnoses often use the term "praxis," which is the ability to do or act. Dyspraxia is difficulty in the ability to do or act; apraxia is the inability to do or act. Dysgraphia is related to translating words to paper, or writing. Dyslexia is related to translating sounds to paper or phonemic awareness; reading and writing. While dysgraphia and dyslexia are considered learning disorders, they are not separate from sensory-processing disorders.

A. Jean Ayres, Ph.D., OTR, and Lucy Jane Miller, Ph.D., OTR/L are among the pioneers in the identification and treatment of sensory-processing disorders. Their work primarily centered around the development of a child's sensory-motor abilities. More recently, new, complementary neuroscience research has been published. A recent study by University of California, San Francisco researchers found differences in the white matter of the brain in children with sensory-processing disorder. "White matter" refers to the myelin-coated nerve fibers in the brain that help all the different parts of the brain communicate and zip information around at the speed of thought. When young subjects with sensory-processing disorder (but without autism or ADHD) were compared to those with no diagnosis, researchers found problems with the white matter in the back of the brain, where the connections involving sensory processing are located. That differs from what has been found in children with ADHD or autism, where white-matter problems tend to be located in the front, or cognitive, part of the brain;. (Anguera, J.A.; Brandes-Aitken, A.N.; Antovich, A.D.; Rolle, C.E.; Desai, S.S.; Marco, E.J., 2017: "A pilot study to determine the feasibility of enhancing cognitive abilities in children with sensory-processing dysfunction.")

Dr. Elysa Marco, a cognitive and behavioral child neurologist, was on the research team to discover the significance that this white matter plays in healthy brain development. Dr. Marco is expanding her research to validate ways that increase white matter, and thereby improve sensory integration. We look forward to the research confirming the current best practices, which include developmental movement and strengthening the ability to focus.

If weak or inefficient neural pathways are one reason for a child's inability to handle certain experiences, it may seem logical that the best remedy would be exposing them to such experiences over and over until they learn how to handle it. However, the fear and stress this causes only serves to reinforce the unwanted patterns and cause further harm. Instead, we must break tasks down into manageable segments, taking one thing at a time, not making one any more significant than the next, and drawing explicit sensory-cognitive connections.

Sensory integration is essential to healthy human development, allowing one to notice, interpret, understand, and respond to the world around them.

All children feel anxious at times; however, children with learning and attention issues are more likely to struggle with fear, stress, and anxiety. It can be expected that children feel anxious in response to a fearful or potentially stressful situation, and generally the anxiety fades when the situation passes or they have successfully navigated the event. Children with anxiety disorders, however, feel anxious most of the time, and often with no specific event or situation that triggers them. Their anxiety also seems more intense or out of proportion to what's going on and often interferes with everyday functioning, especially at school.

Transitions are difficult for most children. When transitions are challenging or produce anxiety, we want to build a child's "transition muscles," metaphorically speaking, helping them to be able to wind down from one activity and be ready for the next activity without undue stress, fear, or anxiety. The first step is to help children trust their environment and the adults around them.

Occupational therapists work to develop optimal alignment, or the optimal position from which to make the next move. For instance, the optimal alignment or starting point from which to roll over is lying down! It makes sense that optimal alignment to run a race, an alert and agile posture, is different from the optimal alignment to learn.

Attempting to transition children from the classroom to lunch recess, or back to class activities, can be chaotic. Caulbridge educators work to strengthen the transition muscle repeatedly throughout the day. For example, as a class time is wrapping up, teachers will cue students that there are a few minutes remaining, reminding the students: "You'll want to finish the sentence you're on now, and begin to put your things away. When your desk is cleared, your pencils and lesson books are inside your desk, and you are sitting quietly, I'll know you're ready to be excused." Once that is accomplished, the teacher cues them for the next step, "Suzie may be excused to line up at the door, Zach is ready, April is ready to line up at the door." When all the children are excused, the teacher waits for a quiet line, then leads them outdoors. Each step of the transition process requires the students' awareness and preparation for the next move, which is meant to strengthen their ability to handle transitions. This practice, which helps to maintain a predictable, calm environment, is in direct contrast to transitions at many schools, where the bell rings, and children dash out to recess like a mob.

Caulbridge educators are thoughtful about creating this place of optimal alignment, where it becomes possible for a child to make the next move with awareness, and oriented to the next activity. When children are disoriented, anxiety builds and they shut down, freeze, or run, resisting the move to the next activity or transition.

Developmental movement is embedded in activities throughout each day to strengthen neural pathways and sensory integration. As a result of the Caulbridge approach, many students with sensory delays will naturally "catch up" and move toward neurotypical – sometimes quite quickly. Children who once became disoriented in transitions can soon move with ease.

IN THE CLASSROOM

Nate had very little body awareness when he came to Caulbridge School, often bumping into people or falling out of his chair. His parents shared that he would rarely react when he fell or hurt himself. This disorganization of his body also translated to a difficulty finding a letter or word on the board, or holding onto multiple pieces of information at a time.

Incorporating developmental movement throughout the day, we watched as Nate's brain/body connection was strengthened and his ability to use his body developed appropriately. Seemingly simple movements, incorporated throughout the day, have a significant impact on the brain/body connection. As his body awareness improved, we saw an increase in his focus and engagement, and he went from struggling with letter recognition to reading beginner high-frequency words.

Your Child's Self-Regulation Is Not Just Self-Control

Self-regulation relates to your child's ability to successfully participate in the classroom, take turns, understand social cues, make good decisions, and be a good friend. Defined as the ability to manage one's behavior, emotions, thoughts, and impulses in the pursuit of long-term goals, self-regulation requires a level of self-awareness and maturity that is capable of delaying gratification.

A child's social-emotional development is cultivated only after they have an experience of connection through caring, mature relationships with adults. It begins with co-regulation, which means a child experiences the adult's sense of calm, understanding, and connection. A child's trust of their world and the adults around them is fundamental to their healthy social-emotional development, which supports self-regulation.

In a sense, we become our children's regulation until they are mature enough for self-regulation. If you're pouring a new sidewalk in the yard, you'll first set up the wooden forms to establish the borders before you mix and pour the concrete. Only when the concrete is set and can stand on its own will you remove the protective forms. Similarly, children will let us know by their behavior if they are able to regulate on their own. We should not assume that when children are not able to regulate that something is wrong; rather, we can know that they still need the form and boundaries of their adult support until their maturity develops.

Focus of attention and regulation of emotions are related. A child who has difficulty with focus will also have challenges with self-regulation. While they are related, the abilities to focus and self-regulate develop differently. Focus correlates with the sensory-motor functions of the brain. Self-regulation, however, is a function of the brain's frontal cortex, which does not mature until about the age of twelve!

Caulbridge pays special attention to the social-emotional and sensory-motor needs of students, developing the ability to focus as a precursor to self-regulation, higher thinking, and ethics. Self-regulation is another component of healthy human development. Regulation results in the ability to calm the nervous system; and to become alert, focused, and available for learning.

Building Your Child's Internal Architecture

Your child's internal architecture refers to their integrity, ethical thinking, initiative, compassion, and awareness. As I was speaking of the importance of these qualities, one parent remarked, "Oh, it's like Jedi training! In the Star Wars world, the Jedi warriors' code emphasizes self-improvement through knowledge and wisdom, and selfless service through acts of charity and citizenship." Well, then yes, it is like Jedi training. Parents should not have to choose between strong academics and strong internal architecture (Jedi training) for their children, and I contend that you cannot really have one without the other.

Twenty years ago, leadership training was about learning strategies for improving performance, management by objective, and getting people to do what you want. Today, much of contemporary leadership training is about developing this internal architecture. Great leaders understand both the art and the science of working with people; they can influence hearts and minds. Great leaders trust their gut. Great leaders have a vision of the world that does not yet exist.

The foundation for this internal architecture begins at an early age and must be built on an underlying sense of trust and safety. In the same way that you would not put a new roof on a building with a shaky foundation, you must first shore up the internal architecture before addressing a child's learning and development.

For the young child, a sense of trust and safety is cultivated through familiar routines, consistency of adult interactions, and plenty of unscheduled time for natural exploration and free play. Trust and safety develop when a child feels respected and heard, understands what is expected of them, and can depend on the structure and boundaries set forth.

We build this internal architecture with:

- Positive relationships
- Structured academics
- Time in nature
- Uncluttered classrooms
- Mindfulness
- Low technology
- Explicit teaching

Compliance: Your Child's Path to Creativity

In the throes of raising children, compliance can get a bad rap. Shouldn't we want our children to be curious and creative, and not blindly comply with what others expect? Children who are unable to do what is asked of them by trusted adults will be unable to do what they ask of themselves.

Once a child practices trust and respect with an adult, they will have an experience upon which to build trust and respect of self and others. Creativity springs forth from a sense of confidence in one's own abilities. Starting with strong attachments to nurturing adults, healthy sensory-motor functions, and sensory processing, children become confident in their own abilities.

Here's how a guided drawing lesson was used to build compliance and the necessary skills that lead to creativity.

During a guided drawing lesson, the teacher at the chalkboard offered step-by-step instructions for drawing a bear. She carefully took the students through the steps of drawing the oval shape for the body, then the head, followed by the arms and legs.

Once the students had the bear on their paper, she asked them to put on their artist hat and add details to the drawing. Maybe there is a forest next to the bear, or flowers in a meadow.

While students were personalizing their drawings, the teacher moved around the class to offer help. She approached Jaden, who scribbled his brown crayon over the entire paper, then pushed the paper away, folded his arms in defiance, and said, "I don't want to draw." Without reacting to his behavior, Jaden's teacher looked at his paper, smiled and said, "Great! Now you have the ground finished. Next let's take this crayon and start on the bear. Where would you like him to be on your paper?" Jaden became engaged, complied and began drawing the bear. He also drew a rock in the bear's hand that he thought might destroy the world, so apparently this bear had super-powers!

Once Jaden became non-compliant, his own creativity shut down. When our actions assume compliance from children, we are teaching them that they are capable of doing what is being asked. Armed with feeling capable and confident, a child's creativity will unfold naturally.

Self-Efficacy or Self-Esteem?

A child's self-efficacy or confidence in their ability to impact the world is directly related to academic and personal success. In her clinical practice treating adolescents, Madeline Levine, Ph.D., psychologist and best-selling author, found that so many of her teenage patients feel empty inside because they lack the secure, reliable, welcoming internal structure that she refers to as "the self." Ms. Levine concludes, "The boredom, the vagueness, unhappiness, and reliance on others, all point to kids who run into difficulty with the very foundation of psychological development."

Dr. Levine offers this distinction: Self-efficacy is the belief that we can successfully impact our world. Unlike self-esteem, which is concerned with judgments of self-worth, self-efficacy is concerned with judgments of personal capability. While self-efficacy often overlaps with self-esteem, it is not the same thing. And unlike self-esteem, which has very little relation to academic, personal, or interpersonal success, self-efficacy has a strong correlation with positive outcomes for children. When children are high in self-efficacy, they find it easy to act on their own behalf. This ability to act appropriately in one's best interest is often called agency.

Self-efficacy refers to beliefs; agency refers to actions; but they both refer to a sense of personal control. Clearly, efficacy and agency are interrelated; the more we believe that we are able to exert control effectively in the world, the more likely we are to act effectively. High levels of agency are found in proactive people, "go-getters" who "know how to get things done." While the term self-efficacy may not be as familiar as self-esteem, it is far more likely to contribute to healthy emotional development.

Children with a healthy self are good architects of their internal "homes," and exhibit the psychological building blocks of self-liking, self-acceptance, and self-management. It is this restorative psychological structure that children need to construct in order to be at ease internally as well as out in the world. Ms. Levine reports that "for many kids in my practice, the internal place of comfort and respite is dangerously underdeveloped."

Caulbridge intentionally supports a child's internal architecture, developing their ability to engage with their ever-changing world.

IN THE CLASSROOM

Noah, an inspired kindergarten student, chose to work during his free time for several days on a story he had begun in class. He would write one sentence per page and illustrate it accordingly. When his story had reached the end, he wrote an "About the Author" page, which stated: "Noah Miller is five years old. He goes to school and lives with his family." He was so proud of his story that he went to his teacher and asked her to make a photocopy so that he could bring it home to his parents.

Less than twelve months ago, Noah avoided any writing activities, since he struggled to even hold his crayon and needed a larger lined space on which to place his letters. Through consistent practice at his skill level, which could vary day to day, we worked to develop Noah's fine motor skills and stamina. We saw his self-efficacy shine through – not only in his writing, but in his attitude towards his learning.

Adam's social anxiety caused him to shy away from social interactions or games on the play yard into which he hadn't been invited. Working with his strengths in the classroom, we found ways to pair Adam with peers and reinforce situations where he could have positive social interactions in a safe environment. That confidence soon transferred to recess time, where Adam boldly walked up to a group of boys playing make-believe and asked, "Can I play with you?" He was delighted by their exuberant yes, grinning from ear-to-ear. His newly developed confidence in his ability to impact the dynamics around him helped to further build his own self-efficacy.

Play – The Essential Nature of Childhood

Play is intrinsic to childhood and fundamental to optimal brain development because it contributes to the cognitive, physical, social, and emotional well-being of children and youth.

Children raised in an increasingly hurried and pressured world are spending less time in unstructured, imaginative play. Less play time means that children are missing essential sensory motor and brain/body connections that naturally develop through movement and play.

Play allows children to create and explore a world they can master, conquering their fears and having power over their conditions. In a child's world, a simple red wand can give them super-powers to save a world from all evil. As they master their world, play helps children develop new competencies, confidence, and the resiliency they will need to face future challenges.

Play is integral to the academic environment. Unstructured play and sufficient time for peer interactions are important components of social-emotional learning in a school setting. Undirected play allows children to learn how to work in groups, to share, to negotiate, to resolve conflicts, and to learn self-advocacy skills. In contrast to passive entertainment, play builds active, healthy bodies and minds.

Play is the single most critical precursor for successful academics. The sensory foundation developed through active, unstructured play is imperative in learning to read and write letters and numbers. Without the sensory-motor foundation, learning will be a challenge. When a child is struggling to understand basic math or reading concepts, it will be important to support the under-developed sensory foundation that academic concepts will be built upon. Even if the child is in fifth grade, they must first build up the basic cognitive and sensory foundation before they will be able to master new learning.

SECTION 2

Traditional Education Systems

Are We Giving Up on Our Children to Accommodate the System?

Accommodations in school are generally offered in response to a student's academic, social-emotional, or physical discrepancies. With rare exception, a student's academic deficits are symptoms of underlying developmental delays, anxieties, sensory-motor or sensory-processing delays.

If a student's academic deficits are related to missed lessons or lack of instruction, then targeted academic remediation may be a simple and relatively quick remedy. However, when those academic struggles correlate with developmental delays, attempting remediation without giving attention to the underlying concerns is short-sighted and ineffective.

For example, a student may show signs of dyspraxia, a lack in coordinated movements and fine motor skills. In school, a child with dyspraxia will have challenges with physical coordination, dexterity, holding a crayon, or handwriting. A typical response to dyspraxia is to simply eliminate handwriting and move to an iPad in an effort to curb a child's frustration and keep them with the class.

Handwriting is often dismissed as a lost art and no longer necessary; however, it is not just about the handwriting. Consider this. Roger Kneebone, a professor of surgical education, is noticing that "Students spend so much time in front of screens, and so little time using their hands, that they have lost the dexterity for stitching or sewing up patients." He understands first-hand that a good surgeon needs dexterity, perception, spatial awareness, and coordination. We all want a surgeon with good hands.

An iPad might accommodate for the immediate struggle with writing; however, it will not make up for the fine motor skills and the eye, hand, and brain coordination developed through the act of handwriting. A complex skill, handwriting engages cognitive, perceptual, and motor skills simultaneously.

Of course, handwriting will be a struggle when fine motor skills are underdeveloped. However, accommodating the immediate frustration without building necessary coordination and dexterity will have consequences throughout a child's school years. More than the obvious consequence of a frustrated child and messy handwriting, not teaching handwriting will result in deficits in reading, spelling, and eye-tracking – to say nothing of the child's self-confidence.

Schools can be quick to offer accommodations that make it easier for teachers to get through the lessons. It is understandable that with large class sizes, students with varying learning needs, and teachers being pressured to deliver content that meets the standards but not always the children, schools must continue to apply Band-Aids or sometimes a tourniquet just to keep marching along.

At Least One in Five Children in Every Classroom Is Affected

Does your child have sensory challenges? Is your child:

- Easily overwhelmed by the environment
- Sensitive to loud noises or scratchy surfaces
- Having difficulty saying goodbye at school
- Struggling with small motor activities like holding a pencil
- Falling a lot or playing too roughly with other children

Children are physical beings who use all their senses to learn. Sensory-processing and learning disorders are on the rise, with a recent study suggesting that one in five children experience sensory challenges sufficient to disrupt their academic, social, and/or emotional development. Teachers in the classroom will tell you those numbers are even higher!

I recently offered a training for the Marin County Early Childhood Directors, who concurred with the dramatic rise in sensory-processing concerns. One preschool director reported that just five years ago, she was seeing one or two among her twenty students who were unable to sit in circle time and had social challenges with peers. Today, she says nineteen out of twenty is no exaggeration!

Learning is a natural process when you integrate nature, arts, movement, friendship, and academics. Time in nature, developmental movement throughout the school day, and artistic activities can work to regulate the nervous system and integrate a child's senses.

Caulbridge understands that children learn best with structure, warmth, and encouragement. Children do not learn when they feel disengaged, anxious, and unsafe, or when the classroom environment is overwhelmed with distraction. Caulbridge works to balance a child's sensory-motor, social-emotional, and academic development. This balance is fundamental to a child's successful school experience.

You Can Teach Focus

An unintended consequence of children growing up in a faster, technology- and media-centered, digitally connected, more-new-now world is that they seem to have shorter attention spans. In response, schools shorten the class periods, setting up almost a game-like environment, with as many as five or eight transitions in an hour! Any teacher will tell you what every parent already knows, that transitions are the most difficult times for young children.

As children show up to school easily distracted, and with shorter attention spans, teachers are vying for the attention of students with fast-moving activities and flashy, almost theatrical lessons. Unfortunately, responding to the symptoms only works to escalate the behaviors, adding to a student's decreased ability to focus. When measuring children's attention skills, across the board, children are performing worse than children of fifty years ago.

A forefather in the field of psychology, William James, author of *The Principles of Psychology,* 1890, included a chapter on attention where he writes, "The faculty of voluntarily bringing back a wandering attention, over and over again, is the very root of judgement, character, and will. An education which should improve this faculty would be *the* education, *par excellence!"*

The ability to focus one's attention is at the core of critical thinking and problem solving. Without it, one becomes reliant on technology or the opinion of others. We see again and again that a child's math won't get in the way of his behavior… but his behavior may get in the way of his math – and indeed, all learning.

Do you want children to develop focus? Teach knife skills.

There are seven rules of knife safety that children must learn before we hand them a carving knife. Stand with your arm fully extended and spin completely around. That is your blood circle, and the first rule of knife safety is: no one can be in your blood circle!

Children respond to being trusted, and will quickly learn any rules necessary to be able to rise up to the exciting challenge.

What about an IEP?

Individualized Education Plans (IEP) are available to public school students with a confirmed disability that limits their access to receiving a basic education. Disabilities like sensory-processing disorders, cognitive delays, emotional disturbance, or health concerns may qualify a child for services provided by the school, free of charge. A team of school personnel along with outside professionals will assess a student, develop recommendations, and work with the child's parents to implement a plan.

While this can be a valuable service for families, students are generally pulled out of class for a remediation lesson or therapy session of some kind. Often these services are disjointed and not coordinated with the regular classroom activities, and only target a specific learning difficulty rather than the whole child. IEP services or accommodations are offered only when a child is struggling and has fallen behind academic expectations by a significant margin. Therefore, a student must *fail* into qualifying for services.

Initially designed for remediation, Universal Design for Learning (UDL) curricula provide the building blocks necessary for students to understand concepts in a concrete manner before moving to the next step. Academic services under an IEP often include one or two sessions per week of tutoring for specific subjects, often math and language arts, using these UDL teaching methods. Students are pulled out of class, then they return to the regular classroom, where the class is being taught in a completely different way using a different curriculum.

Caulbridge uses a UDL math and language arts platform for everyone, so that all students receive structured, scaffolded academics every day. For math and language arts at Caulbridge, students are grouped by skill level rather than grade level, so students are not removed from their classmates.

One or two occupational-therapy or speech-therapy sessions per week are also typical accommodations in traditional schools. Students are pulled from class time to work with practitioners on specific skills. Caulbridge, on the other hand, incorporates developmental movement into all aspects of the day, with children spending time in nature, hiking, building, digging – all activities that intentionally address the proprioceptive, spatial-awareness, and bilateral coordination needs of the developing child.

The traditional school student population consists of about 50% of children who are considered typical learners and 50% of children experiencing learning differences, sensory-processing delays, anxieties, or attention-deficit disorder. Remaining together as a class has great value in helping to create a picture of expected behaviors, and provides lots of opportunities to practice new behaviors, adding to the social dynamics and helping to develop friendships.

Classrooms where the range of behavior and learning differences is not acknowledged only serves to perpetuate learning struggles for students until their behavior is cause for removal from the class. Inclusive classrooms, on the other hand, can support children by managing classroom expectations and differentiating lessons to meet a wider range of student needs.

After a successful preschool experience, Dylan entered kindergarten at the local public school and immediately reacted to the environment. He was sent home early every day because of his emotional outbursts and resistance to participation. Due to the severity of his behaviors, the school initiated an IEP process for him. Dylan's IEP goals and interventions related to the identified symptoms and behaviors exhibited at school, such as emotional disruption, attention deficits, and defiant behaviors.

Just a few weeks into the school year, Dylan's parents removed him from the public school system and inquired about enrollment at Caulbridge. Our admissions process includes a review of the student's records, communication with his previous school (including preschool), and an invitation for Dylan to visit the school for a "shadow day" in order for our teachers to have a first-hand observation of his behavior. Within hours, it was clear that Dylan's reactive and sometimes explosive behaviors were in response to his previous school environment. Given a different environment where he felt safe, he could have a positive school experience.

As part of the IEP process, the local school district was required to observe Dylan at his new school. Mr. Jensen, the Behavior Health Specialist, spent a total of six hours observing Dylan, in two-hour blocks of time, spread over several days and at varying times of the day to get a full perspective of the school experience. During his observation, Mr. Jensen couldn't believe the change he saw in just a few weeks. He reported that the student had no signs of the behaviors they had observed in the former public-school setting, and he had no academic, social, or behavior concerns for the child. Mr. Jensen added that he wished every child could have this kind of education!

Technology

Sometimes, in an effort to accelerate children's learning, we may inadvertently be doing them a disservice. I was interviewed by Nicholas Kardaras, Ph.D., for his bestselling book, *Glow Kids*, which examines how screen addiction is hijacking our kids. Here's an excerpt from the book:

"The argument for technology in the earlier grades is often rooted in the fear of children falling behind. It is true that most children will use technology in their jobs and everyday life. It is also true that most children will learn to drive a car," Debra told me. *"Certainly we would not give a 7-year-old child the car keys to give them a jump-start to be a more skillful driver. In the same way, we want to ensure children can effectively use technology as a tool and will bring all of their best thinking, creativity and innovation to bear."*

An increasing body of literature shows that today's fast-paced technology and media-infused society can negatively influence the development of children on many levels, including reducing their capacity to create a meaningful connection with others and the world around them. Increased technology and social media use does correlate with the rise in sensory-processing and learning disorders, anxieties, mood disorders, and depression among children.

When overloaded, adults can unplug – spend some down time to refocus their thoughts, adjust their mood, reflect on their behavior, and respond accordingly. Children cannot.

Justin's mother approached me after school and said, "I think I know what you're going to say, but what's the research about the effects of video games on children?"

Knowing she has a six-year-old, and an older brother who loved video games, I asked, "What's your experience? What do you notice about your children?"

She shook her head. "Well, I definitely see a difference in my boys when they play video games. It's as if they are fixated and don't hear anything else. The flashing lights and sounds have them mesmerized. They don't sleep as well, they can't concentrate on anything else, they are moodier and even more aggressive!"

Without knowing the specific research, this mother was living her own case study and seeing first-hand all the consequences borne out by the research.

It is not uncommon to hear parents speaking about the struggles with their child's technology habits, knowing it is disruptive or even harmful to the child, and yet not feeling empowered to manage the technology use in the home. This can be compounded when young children are expected to have their own devices or use technology in the classroom.

Another mother asked if educational video games help children learn. "How is it that my child is struggling to pay attention in school but can figure out how to play these games, remembering all the rules and even the strange names of the characters?"

Taking a page from the game-theory playbook, we can see the elements of effective teaching! Video games are built on the premise that you must first master one skill level before moving on to the next. Each new level of skill is connected to the previous, building upon what the player knows and advancing the degree of difficulty. This is all good, and very effective. Unfortunately, it's not the whole picture. What is missing in learning from video games is the sensory-motor and brain development necessary for healthy child development.

Caulbridge engages the young child in adult and peer interactions, rather than using computer screens for learning. There is no regular use of technology in the lower grades, except for students with special needs who may benefit from assistive technology for learning.

Technology is used as a tool to enhance children's work and creativity in the older grades. Media literacy, digital citizenship, online safety and ethics are essential as students enter pre-adolescence and middle school.

SECTION 3

What Is Really Going On?

How Children Learn – The Neuroscience of Learning

In simple terms, the brain develops from the back to the front; from the base of the skull up toward the forehead. First to come online are the lower-level senses, physical growth and physiological development, reflexes, sensory and motor functions. Next to activate is the mid-brain area, where the limbic system governs trust, emotions, instincts, and aesthetics. Last to develop is the frontal cortex, which is the area of reasoning, problem solving, and higher-level critical thinking.

If you look at a child's brain, in these familiar images of the motor centers in the brain you see the centers that control critical thinking, spatial movements, and executive functioning. These control centers are pretty much developed at birth. What is NOT developed are the neural pathways and connections *between* the centers. These pathways are developing at an astronomical rate before the age of five, are not fully developed until the age of twenty-five, and luckily for us, are being regenerated throughout our adult life!

It may seem counterintuitive that developing a solid foundation does not require stimulation of the control centers, but rather the development of the neural pathways.

Healthy development of neural pathways requires three things:

- Movement of the body
- Nature
- Human interaction

Things that interrupt or interfere with the healthy neural pathway development include over- or under-stimulation of the senses through too much technology, toxins, or trauma.

As babies take in information through the senses, their brain cells (or neurons) respond by creating connections – neural pathways – with each other. These pathways resemble an electrical wiring system. Each neural pathway is a circuit. Each neuron can have multiple connections within different neural pathways inside this complex brain development.

Neurons carry messages or thoughts in the form of electrical signals called nerve impulses. To create a nerve impulse, neurons have to be activated or excited. Stimuli such as light, sound, or pressure all excite the neurons, releasing chemicals that will trigger a nerve impulse.

Brain chemicals (neurotransmitters) such as adrenaline, dopamine, serotonin, and norepinephrine help power the system and move messages through the brain circuitry. These brain chemicals trigger a response just as electricity powers a response when it goes through a circuit.

Synapse

Neuron

Your Child's Neuro Signature

Some brain circuits, like the ones for breathing and circulation, are developed at birth. Other brain circuits are "activity-dependent" and need inputs that a child receives through their sensory experiences. Touch, sounds, sights, tastes, and smells, along with the qualities of their environment, all initiate the brain's neurotransmitters and power circuits to build neural pathways. The network of neural connections between motor areas and biological systems is the basis for a child's neuro-development.

Neural pathways begin as spider web-like connections that rely on repetition to build into stronger networks. Circuits that are not used weaken and disappear over time through a process known as "pruning," which continues through adolescence and beyond. Young children have more circuits than they need, and children's brains are flexible enough to work continuously to build new circuits and refine commonly used neural pathways. This is known as "plasticity."

Your child's neuro-development becomes their unique signature, which serves as the basis for future behavior and learning.

Explicit Teaching: Old-Fashioned or Essential?

Children are bombarded with sensory inputs that are taxing their memory processing and shutting down their ability to turn information into knowledge and skills.

Academic and cognitive development require both long-term memory and working memory. Long-term memory includes everything from the addition facts we just learned yesterday to knowledge accumulated over our lifetime.

There are two kinds of long-term memory:

1. Procedural memory – sometimes referred to as muscle memory – where information, such as how to ride a bike, is stored in the body and becomes automatic.

2. Memories of general knowledge, including facts or events that involve conscious thought and learning.

Working memory refers to the intake and processing of new information. Processing new information, such as combinations of numbers or letters, can only be stored in the working memory for brief periods of time (minutes or even seconds), and is limited in the amount of information that can be processed.

You may have experienced resistance when your child is uncertain or lacks confidence. Whether that resistance shows up as frustration, quitting, blaming, or pretending to know something then becoming argumentative – these are all indications that their working-memory processing is on overload and no new learning can occur. When overloaded, sensory and memory processing go into survival mode, "fight or flight," and the child cannot learn.

Research shows that students learn more deeply from strongly guided learning than from discovery. In spite of the research, most traditional schools work from a constructivist model, based in the idea that if we can interest children in a subject, they'll begin to pick up the processes on their own. Progressive education relies on an inquiry-based methodology, believing that if children discover their own answers, it will have more relevance and long-lasting learning. Minimal guidance, or letting young children discover answers for themselves, however, places a huge burden on the working memory. We may think that by taxing the working memory, we are helping to strengthen it – but the opposite is true; we are actually overloading the working memory to the point of ineffectiveness.

What about a child's imagination and natural curiosity? For the young child, it is the explicit teaching that builds trust of themselves, and their world, which actually strengthens their imagination, curiosity, and creativity.

Only with guided instruction can children learn to effectively process new information and commit it to long-term memory, where it is possible to access the information and act on it. Children first learn to trust themselves and their world when the adults around them are capable. The more predictability and stability in the environment, the more deeply a child can trust. Effective teaching is explicit, and gives children specific guidance about how to understand and manipulate information in ways that capture and store the result in long-term memory.

Teaching Kids to Love What They Hate – Executive Functioning

You may have heard your child insist "I hate math," or "I'm not good at reading." Learning is a natural process for children, so when they resist learning, they may be telling us something much more significant than personal preference. They may be letting us know they do not have the executive functioning skills to understand what we're asking. Dismissing these symptoms as someone who "is just not a math person" would be a disservice, and this may perpetuate compensation strategies that are likely to cause further problems down the road.

Executive functioning is more than being organized. Executive-function skills include the ability to stop and think before acting (impulse control), the ability to regulate or manage one's emotional life, and the ability to mentally hold a picture and manipulate information or working memory. While generally not taught in the classroom, these skills are essential for academic success. When these foundational skills are underdeveloped, giving a child an organizer – even a beautiful, color-coded organizer – is not likely to result in more-effective prioritizing or focus. Increasing the child's working-memory process, however, will help build their executive-functioning skills.

If there was a water bottle that spilled, it was probably Danny's! Chaos seemed his natural state. His mother often complained that he was not able to find anything, and they were chronically late because Danny was "on his own time schedule." Danny found it difficult to focus, and he was impulsive. Danny's working memory was on overload, and his spatial awareness was underdeveloped.

Clear, explicit instruction helps to minimize the load on a child's working memory, which improves focus and learning. At Caulbridge, we help strengthen Executive Functioning by giving students quality materials that they are responsible for taking care of. Students have a pouch for their crayons, a bin for their colored pencils, a drawer for their lesson book. Students' materials only come out when it is time to use them for class, and the children put them away when finished. By being responsible for and taking care of their materials, the children develop spatial awareness and organizational skills.

SECTION 4

Education for Our Time

Building the Code of Learning – From Concrete to Abstract

Typically, when children struggle with academics, it is not because they lack the intelligence or even the desire to learn, but rather are missing the foundational skills and basic tools.

If a child is not taught explicitly, in a code-oriented, linear pattern, they are not receiving the basics they need to master the concepts of math or reading. Evidence reveals that explicit, direct instruction, taught in a systematic way, works to build the codes of math, language arts, and all learning.

When you first learned double-digit addition, you may have learned to "carry the one" when the numbers were greater than nine. Except it's not a one, it's a ten that needs to be carried. Adding thirty-eight plus twenty-four means you are creating a new ten, and you now have a two in the ones place. This example of a simple misunderstanding of number values leads to some of the most common math mistakes. As calculations become more advanced, these mistakes compound.

Math and Language Arts at Caulbridge are inspired by Universal Design for Learning (UDL), which is a set of principles for curriculum development that provides skills for all children, regardless of learning style. A solid foundation in literacy and numeracy builds both competence and confidence, which can turn a child's natural curiosity into a love of learning. These UDL academic programs are often used for remediation when children missed the foundational skills in reading or math; however, we want all children to develop solid skills and not wait to remediate.

Learning moves from very concrete concepts to the more abstract. While there are different ways of *processing* information, everyone *learns* the same way.

An example of this progression can be seen in the way we teach math at Caulbridge:

1. Build numbers using manipulatives with color-coded, place-value boxes (concrete)

2. Record the number with color-coded, place-value boxes (concrete)

3. Progress to building numbers using manipulatives with recording boxes that are not color coded (semi-concrete)

4. Move to recording numbers without manipulatives still in the boxes (semi-abstract),

5. Finally, record numbers without the boxes or other supports (abstract).

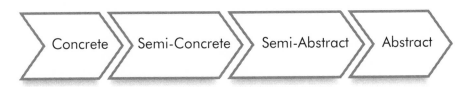

Building the code of learning in this way creates a solid foundation upon which higher-level concepts will eventually rest. If we notice regression in a student's skills as math concepts progress, we know to go back and shore up their foundational skills in order to move forward. For example, when students begin working with addition and subtraction and flip the place value of their teens (i.e. 17 becomes 71), we know that they need to go back to the place-value boxes and reset their mental picture or symbol imaging of these numbers.

All learning – not just mathematics – must progress in this way, from concrete to abstract. For instance, for a young child, the concept of "sharing" is highly abstract. We often ask children to be nice and share toys with their friend – not an easy idea. Teaching a child to take turns is a more concrete and manageable concept. "It is my turn" is very concrete.

The progression of a child learning to share may look like this:

1. Taking turns with adult support. (concrete)

2. Taking turns without adult support (semi-concrete)

3. Playing together but having distinct turns with a toy (semi-abstract)

4. Playing with the toy together. Sharing. (abstract).

Strong literacy and numeracy require the integration of key cognitive skills such as symbol imaging, detail analysis, and sequential processing within every lesson and activity. That means having the ability to recognize a number or letter symbol and what it represents.

Everyone learns using the concrete-to-abstract process. While there are different ways of processing information, everyone learns the same way. The concrete-to-abstract structure is vital. It takes a student through the concrete stage (using manipulatives or blocks) to the abstract stage (numbers on the page) with precise management of manipulatives and precise language, all the while activating the key areas of the brain necessary for students to connect and understand the symbolic form (abstract) of math. Starting with mastery at the concrete level of learning, it requires incremental steps to move the learning to semi-concrete, then semi-abstract, before moving finally to abstract learning.

Math requires good executive-function skills. If your child struggles in the area of executive function, it is paramount to their math success to reduce the load on their working memory. Using supports such as manipulatives and color-coding help to build the code of information while supporting the working memory and executive-functioning skills.

It Starts Around Third Grade

Academics tend to break down around third grade, when children go from learning-to-read to reading-to-learn, or from simple arithmetic to more complex math concepts. In the earlier grades it is more likely that learning differences will go unnoticed, because children are quick to develop compensation strategies. As the learning becomes more complex, these strategies tend to fall apart. For example, it may appear that a student is reading, when they have actually memorized the sentences. As soon as the reading demand becomes too great to simply memorize, a student will become overwhelmed and resistant to reading.

Whenever I hear a well-meaning adult helping with homework say to a child, "I'm going to show you a trick," I shudder because it generally means they are offering a procedural trick without the necessary comprehension behind it. Instead, when a child is struggling, they likely need the concepts broken down further, more concretely, rather than layering a trick over the misunderstanding.

While it starts around third grade, these learning challenges are not without warning signs that are evident as early as kindergarten. A strong foundation for academics requires an understanding of one-to-one correspondence, and the ability to decode and encode (break down and build up) numbers and symbols. This number-symbol relationship is developed in direct correlation to the natural physical and sensory developments of the child. Building a strong picture of numbers and symbols can help to activate and sustain working memory and other brain processes necessary for more-advanced learning. Working memory also correlates to spatial awareness, balance, and imagination.

Children with underdeveloped working memory may appear scattered, have poor motor control, and be drawn to sensory-seeking behaviors like fidgeting, pushing, or rough play. When these foundational skills are underdeveloped, giving a child a "trick" is *not* likely to result in more-effective learning. Building proprioceptive capacity – also known as spatial awareness – in support of working memory, however, *will* in turn support academics.

Rather than waiting until third grade to identify learning challenges, Caulbridge works to build the code of learning that is sustainable as children move through their school years.

What is Developmental Movement and Why Does My Child Need It?

Children learn through the senses, and through movement of the body, which starts initially as the involuntary reflexes of a baby. These early reflexes organize the brain for vision and hearing, as well as for learning, attention, and emotional balance. Clusters of reflexes generate developmental movements that help to build and organize neurological connections for the brain. Immature reflexes affect sensory inputs, body awareness, focus, and learning.

While these reflexes tend to progress naturally, children can also get stuck in a particular pattern that prevents them from progressing to fully integrating sensory experiences. Those patterns can also affect the brain's capacity to advance to higher learning. The good news is that the brain responds quickly to movements (i.e., jumping, balancing, crossing the midline, posture and coordination activities, gross and fine motor skills) that naturally support a child's underdeveloped sensory processing or brain/body connection.

Research has shown that children who have immature reflexes have a higher incidence of specific learning difficulties compared to children with mature reflexes, and that using developmental movement to support the appropriate reflexes toward maturation correlates with improvements in reading and writing.

Caulbridge understands that movement = learning. One of our Three Foundational Principles is that *Learning is Physiological and Begins in the Body*. More than simple exercise, developmental movement helps calm the nervous system, balance emotions, and organize the sensory inputs that build a healthy brain/body connection. This strong foundation of learning in the early grades prepares the brain for more-abstract thinking and higher-level reasoning. For optimal learning, developmental movement practices are intentionally embedded in student activities throughout our school day.

Kids Are ALWAYS on Their Best Behavior

Surely, a child yelling "I hate you," or throwing shoes around the room, is not demonstrating their best behavior. But in that moment, yes, they are.

Infants will cry to let us know they are hungry, or need help to meet their needs. Toddlers may use simple words and gestures. With time, children learn to communicate their thoughts and needs. Sometimes they use direct language, spoken with kindness – and other times they might scream or run and hide. Sometimes a tantrum is the only way to express helplessness, anxiety, or overwhelm – at these times, a tantrum is genuinely the child's best behavior. Either the child is so distraught that they can't find any other way to express their frustration, or they have learned that a tantrum is actually the quickest way to get what they want. Even as adults, when we become tired, hungry, or anxious, our behavior may be different than when we are rested and have some perspective.

We never want to assume the child "knows better." In fact, in this moment, they are demonstrating that they do not. Even if just yesterday they behaved differently, today it is clear they need more practice.

Even when it feels as if the child's behavior is manipulative, or they are just trying to get their way, we must not assume their behavior is directed at us personally. What feels like manipulation may actually be a healthy attempt at social referencing. Just as a laughing toddler running ahead of the slower adult will turn and check to see the adult is still there, children will "check in" with adults they have an attachment to as they test their own physical and behavioral boundaries.

All behavior is the reflection of a child's skills, limitations, emotions, and moods within any given environment. It becomes our job as the adults to interpret the behavior and either reinforce it or shift the behavior toward healthy development. What is this behavior taking care of? We can offer a better way for the child to respond, then help them to practice new behaviors.

As parents and educators, when we start by assuming the child's behavior is their best solution, we can more clearly identify the problem and provide the best response.

Caulbridge educators view all behavior as information. Students who are dysregulated cannot learn. Whenever a student becomes dysregulated, triggered, or anxious we check for three things:

1. Are they safe?

2. Are they connected to themselves or someone else?

3. Do they have the skills and capacities they need?

First, we determine if they need to be shielded from a situation. Then we establish a connection with the child so they feel cared about and know there is an adult who can help. Only after we determine that the child is safe, and is connected to an adult, do we determine what new skill or reminder is needed to shift their current behavior and practice new ones.

Through this lens, we see what is in the way of a child's learning, and first re-regulate the child before attempting to address the behavior. Connection before correction! This perspective also helps us to remain neutral and not be personally triggered by the acting-out behavior. With an objective perspective, it is more likely that we can help guide the child toward a new behavior that may add to the child's positive development.

SECTION 5

The Caulbridge Solution

A New Education Paradigm

Our country's current school system remains locked into an education paradigm that is no longer relevant for our time. At the core of the problem is that learning has been reduced to the mere accumulation of information, rote responses focusing on the "right" answer, fragmented subject matter, and irrelevant testing methods that are often unrelated to a child's developmental stage.

Yet all is not lost. Current research and collective wisdom provide us with the information and methods necessary for any child to receive a sound, healthy education. Caulbridge leads the way in providing a new model of elementary education. In developing our common sense education, we deeply examined both learning and childhood and believe schools must move from:

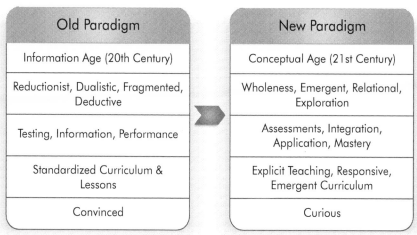

Old Paradigm	New Paradigm
Information Age (20th Century)	Conceptual Age (21st Century)
Reductionist, Dualistic, Fragmented, Deductive	Wholeness, Emergent, Relational, Exploration
Testing, Information, Performance	Assessments, Integration, Application, Mastery
Standardized Curriculum & Lessons	Explicit Teaching, Responsive, Emergent Curriculum
Convinced	Curious

The old education paradigm relates back to the industrial age, when education functioned as a training ground for future factory workers. Schools decided what skills children should have, then fit students into the education system without much allowance for those who learned differently or who had different needs. In some ways, this was an efficient and even tidy process to create the necessary and well-trained factory worker. With the changing needs of our children and world, it becomes imperative to re-examine everything we once assumed about education.

Where once schools and parents had similar goals and expectations for children, it now seems that parents' hopes and priorities for their children have moved beyond the child "getting the right job" to focusing on achieving an overall high quality of life. Parents seem frustrated by current school choices: specifically, the lack of a nurturing environment, the high-pressured intensity of academics, the overuse of technology, lack of healthy social climates, lack of professionalism in teachers, and lack of integrity and transparency.

Representing the new paradigm, Caulbridge focuses on child development and works to develop a child's social-emotional, sensory-motor, and academic skills. This paradigm supports both a sound education and a high quality of life.

When I asked a young couple what attracted them to Caulbridge, the dad simply said, "We don't want the light in our son's eyes to dim." They were looking for a relevant education in a nurturing environment.

Common Sense Education

In these unprecedented times of change and uncertainty, we cannot begin to know the world our children will inherit. How, then, do we trust that we are effectively preparing them?

A common sense education begins with the child in mind. It asks what is needed for healthy childhood development, and how we teach the cognitive, social-emotional, and sensory-motor skills in a balanced way. This becomes a strong foundation for learning. Since it is impossible to know what skills will be needed in their lifetime, we must equip students with the mindset, skillset, and internal architecture to navigate their world.

Cognitive skills are the ability to think, reason, and learn. Children learn by moving from an explicit, concrete picture to the more abstract concepts in a direct, step-by-step way that builds on prior understanding. Children may process differently; however, everyone learns the same way – first understanding concepts concretely, then moving to the abstract. Strong academics require hands-on, experiential activities and continued practice.

Social-emotional skills are the ability to understand one's emotional life and to relate to others. When children feel safe and trust their environment, they learn to interact positively with others. A school environment of healthy rhythms and clear expectations helps children be confident and capable. This confidence in their own abilities extends to relating to others, to learning, and to their world.

Sensory-motor skills are the abilities to receive and process information, then to respond or act accordingly. The healthy development of a child's senses, spatial awareness, bilateral coordination, and working memory are at the core of learning.

Your Child's Hierarchy of Needs for School Success

The chart below compares the basic needs for human development and a child's school success.

Maslow's Hierarchy of Needs reminds us that only when the basic physiological and safety needs are met can one develop a healthy self-concept and achieve self-actualization.

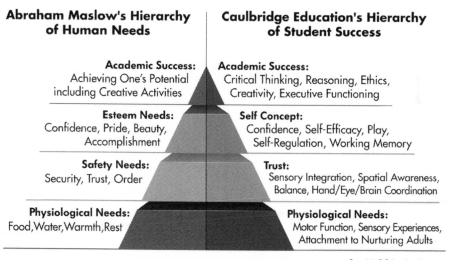

Abraham Maslow's Hierarchy of Human Needs	Caulbridge Education's Hierarchy of Student Success
Academic Success: Achieving One's Potential including Creative Activities	**Academic Success:** Critical Thinking, Reasoning, Ethics, Creativity, Executive Functioning
Esteem Needs: Confidence, Pride, Beauty, Accomplishment	**Self Concept:** Confidence, Self-Efficacy, Play, Self-Regulation, Working Memory
Safety Needs: Security, Trust, Order	**Trust:** Sensory Integration, Spatial Awareness, Balance, Hand/Eye/Brain Coordination
Physiological Needs: Food, Water, Warmth, Rest	**Physiological Needs:** Motor Function, Sensory Experiences, Attachment to Nurturing Adults

Copyright © D. Lambrecht

Caulbridge works to meet the foundational sensory-motor and social-emotional needs in support of sound academic development. Without a child's basic sense that their world is a safe place, or a well-developed body/brain connection, learning will be a struggle. Intellectual and cognitive capacities develop naturally from a child's well-integrated sensory experiences and body awareness, along with gross and fine motor skills. The ability to learn is based on this hierarchy – whether to be a friend, build a birdhouse, or learn to read.

Once trust and respect are practiced with an adult, a child will have an experience upon which to build trust and respect of themselves and others. Creativity springs forth from a sense of confidence in one's abilities. Building confidence in children begins with strong attachments to nurturing adults, with healthy sensory-motor functions and sensory processing.

Caulbridge resists the trend to skip over essential childhood brain development for more simple and short-sighted goals, because to skip over any of these distinct areas will have dire consequences as a child moves through their school years.

Raising Children, Not Test Scores

When my daughter was twelve years old, we bought a new house with a beautiful yard. The gardener, Mikel, had been mowing the grass and tending the flowers at this house for years, so when we moved in, he came by to see if we would be continuing with his services. As I declined, he suggested that without his services, "we were not going to raise good grass." I replied that I'm not raising grass, I'm raising a daughter – and I want to instill a work ethic in her. Mikel loved that idea and completely supported my decision. He often stopped by when he was working in the neighborhood to say hi, or to bring some wonderful homemade Basque treats.

Academic success takes good old hard work. Children can learn to focus their attention and see a task through to completion, even when it feels like hard work. Believe me, once my daughter got older and hard work came naturally to her, I hired a gardener!

Hard work, initiative, and confidence are among several qualities that link directly to academic success. In the early 1990s I served on the board of directors for the Center for Applied Research Solutions, a non-profit organization focused on youth research and best practices for the prevention community, practitioners, policy makers, and the public. The organization was instrumental in the facilitation of research and survey data – conducted by the SEARCH Institute – that identified both internal strengths and external supports in young people, which they called developmental assets. The survey measured these developmental assets and correlated them to academic, social-emotional, and personal success. Internal strengths measured were things like commitment to learning, personal values, social competencies, and self-esteem.

External supports were identified as children being valued and receiving support from adults at home, school, and community, along with having clear expectations and boundaries.

Over time, studies of more than 5 million young people consistently show that the more developmental assets young people have, the less likely they are to engage in a wide range of high-risk behaviors and the more likely they are to thrive. Specifically, children with the most assets are more likely to:

- Do well in school
- Be civically engaged
- Value diversity

Youth with the least amount of assets are more likely to have problems with:

- Alcohol and drug use
- Violence
- Sexual activity

In 1994, I was invited to present my ideas to the United Nations at their International Drug Controle Programme: *Developing an International Strategy Conference*. Each panelist had just six minutes, so I cut right to the chase and opened with, "I don't think we have an alcohol and drug problem in our country – I think we have an alcohol and drug solution!"

As human beings, we have a need to connect, to share experiences, and to care about each other and our world. When children grow up without unconditional love, clear boundaries, and adult support, they often find their own solution by using alcohol, drugs, or other risky behaviors to numb the pain and anxiety of feeling unsafe in the world.

Now, twenty-five years later, this concept remains relevant as we move to empower our children to use new, healthier solutions. Schools play a crucial role in raising each generation of children. To focus solely on raising test scores is to neglect the real needs of children, which will ultimately result in diminished academic and personal success.

The child-development perspective of Caulbridge education builds on every child's internal strengths and external supports in support of their academic and personal success.

Teaching, Learning, and Measuring What Matters

In these unprecedented times of change and uncertainty, preparing children to be adaptive thinkers with strength of heart and character is essential. Schools must go beyond the basic academic testing in order to prepare young people for their real future. When teaching is explicit and scaffolded using clear supports, and when learning expectations are developmentally appropriate, measuring a child's progress will more likely produce accurate, meaningful assessments that measure what matters.

In the beginning, Caulbridge identified student outcomes. We also identified the assessments and metrics that will inform the curriculum and teaching activities. Our goal is to align outcomes with process. Learning outcomes drives student assessments and results, not the other way around. If teachers are teaching one thing, yet the school district is assessing something else, teachers will feel pressured to conform to the assessment requirements rather than the students' needs. It is, therefore, critical to determine what matters and how to measure what matters.

Academics matter. It can be easy to push academics aside as less important than the character education or people skills a child will need in the "real" world. From our child-development perspective, academics and life skills are equally important, and one cannot be fully achieved without the other.

Children are naturally inquisitive; their brains and bodies develop naturally toward new capacities and new learning. If a child is struggling with academics, something is in the way. These struggles are a red flag, and they become an obvious point of assessment or exploration. Beyond numeracy and literacy skills, Math and Language Arts help to build the code of learning. The neural pathways built through the study of academics help to support the brain circuitry for higher-level reasoning and sound logic. To dismiss a child's difficulty in picking up their early math facts as unimportant or easily compensated with a calculator is to miss the critical brain development for higher reasoning.

Caulbridge assessments are aligned to grade-level expectations, along with a child's capacities and learning styles, and they ultimately help to inform the ongoing teaching and learning needs. Rather than standardized testing, Caulbridge uses curriculum-referenced tests, along with portfolio- and observation-style academic assessments. Comprehensive developmental assessments that include academic, sensory-motor, and social-emotional development offer a more complete picture of a child's education.

In addition to measuring academics, sensory-motor and social-emotional skills, Caulbridge has committed to an in-depth assessment process.

We measure:

1. Observation skills
2. Courageous learning
3. Positive self-concept

These three student outcomes reflect the core beliefs and priorities of Caulbridge Education.

Peter Poutiatine, a prominent educator and evaluation consultant, worked with the Caulbridge team to help design high-quality assessment metrics that measure what matters most for student success. Mr. Poutiatine consults with schools across the country and serves as the Senior School Selection Coordinator of George Lucas Education Foundation's Edutopia.

"That's what is so great about what Caulbridge is doing," declared Mr. Poutiatine. "Observation skills, courageous learning, and positive self-concept: these are what it takes to show up, understand what is happening, jump in, and start making change for the good of the community. I think we are a bit ahead of the curve, and truly that is what it is to be leading, breaking trail."

Observation skills are essential to be able to assess a situation and to solve problems.

Observation is the ability to perceive details in one's environment and to ascribe meaning to what is perceived. By perceive, we mean the ability to receive information through the senses, then process and act upon those inputs to construct perceptions. Observation happens within all environments: the physical, natural, cultural, and human surroundings. Meaning is ascribed by arriving at inferences and conclusions in reasonable, creative, and intuitive ways.

IN THE CLASSROOM

Each spring our students' observation skills, as well as their ability to sit and focus, has greatly increased. Why? Lizards.

Nothing will teach observation and focus better than lizards! When the sun warms the rocks in the yard and the lizards come out to sun bathe, you'll find our students quiet, still, and working together to find, watch, and coax lizards onto their open hands. Using their observation skills, the students assess where the lizard would be sun bathing, where it might run if frightened, and if the lizard is calm enough to approach or if it's showing signs of distress.

Courageous learning is identified as a student outcome because the ability to step outside of one's comfort zone is a critical skill that relates to success in academics, relationships, and life.

Courage does not imply a lack of fear or concern for the outcome. Courage is the willingness to proceed *despite* one's concern, and in the presence of one's fear. Action without concern for the outcome might be deemed recklessness. The notion of risk is highly personal, contextual, developmental, and cultural. Courage must be understood in regard to each of those areas.

Accepting an emotional risk means embracing the potential to have uncomfortable feelings as the result of an action or experience – stepping outside of one's comfort zone.

A social risk requires embracing the potential for uncomfortable interactions with other people as a result of an action or experience.

By accepting an intellectual risk, we embrace the potential of having to change one's mind or shift one's understanding as the result of an action or experience.

IN THE CLASSROOM

On Wilderness Day, Jenny was struggling through a dense deer trail, getting stuck in blackberry vines and fighting her way over fallen branches. A first grader, she seemed frustrated and helpless as she struggled up the trail. She was less than eager when we had to turn back and travel down the same path. But once she learned how to interact with her environment, studying the patterns of how the branches were growing, and discovering the berries on the blackberry bushes, she found her confidence and joy. She exclaimed, "I LOVE THIS! I couldn't do it before, but now I can – and I love this!"

This is courageous learning, the ability to learn from and overcome obstacles and challenges. In this situation, her courage was met with a sweet surprise. Days later, in a challenging math lesson, she only had to be reminded of the blackberry experience and she was able to use her courage to break down the problem and successfully complete her work.

Upon transferring to Caulbridge, Paul learned that there would be gardening and earth sciences lessons that involved excavating in the yard. Paul was terrified to touch dirt or anything found there. He adopted the role of observer and relied on the support of his partner, who willingly took on the digging. Paul's anxiety about dirt and bugs could often haunt him, leaving him feeling as if things were crawling on his skin. Always given the option to observe, Paul watched his classmates' enthusiasm for finding worms in the garden beds, their delight at lizards basking in the sun, and their joy of just digging in the dirt. Within weeks of settling into his new school, Paul went from an observer to a participant who discovers beetles by the handful. At the end of the day, he's one of the dirtiest, happiest kids in class.

Paul's anxiety decreased and his courage increased with the unconditional support he received. While he always tried his best to be a good student, his anxiety was a barrier to learning. The courage it took to meet new challenges in the garden transferred to the classroom.

Positive self-concept serves as a source of resiliency and compassion for self and others in times of increased stress or challenging situations.

By positive self-concept we mean the ability to evaluate oneself in positive and self-affirming ways across situations and contexts, even when falling short of one's expectations or hopes; the ability to demonstrate pro-social behavior, ethical decision-making, and a striving for genuine and caring relationships.

Teaching Through the Senses

Thought begins with a sensory stimulus, further underscoring the importance of healthy sensory integration. Children are physical beings who absorb, interpret, process, and act on information through the senses. Sensory stimuli such as light, sound, or pressure all ignite neurons, releasing chemicals that trigger a nerve impulse. The nerve impulses are electrical signals that carry information, thoughts, or messages. Delays in sensory processing and incoherent sensory cognitive connections will prove challenging in all areas of a child's life, including friendships and school.

Using the chart below, we follow examples from sensory experiences to behavior. While this can happen so quickly as to seem entirely random, all behavioral responses can be tracked back to the sensory interpretation and processing of the incident.

Senses	Intellectual Response	Emotional Response	Behavioral Response
- See, Hear, Touch, Taste, Smell - Body senses: Vestibular (balance) - Proprioceptive (Muscles, Spatial Awareness) - Interoceptive (organs, sensations)	Think	Feel	Act / Do

Copyright © D. Lambrecht

Imagine it's dinner time with your family. You've spent the day cleaning the house and preparing for a special family dinner, when your four-year-old spills her milk across the entire table. You become startled, seeing milk puddling on the roasted chicken dish and drenching the salad. You hear her cup hit the floor, and milk dripping onto the floor. Your daughter is upset, and her brother is yelling that it wasn't his fault. Your thoughts are racing, "Of all nights – I worked on a new recipe for tonight, and I just cleaned these floors." You react, shouting, "I told you to use two hands!"

In this all-too-familiar example, the thinking, feeling, and behavior responses do not match the incident. Another more objective and appropriate response might be to clean up the milk, and engage the children in helping as they can. What a perfect teachable moment for learning a more appropriate response to literally "crying over spilled milk."

When a child is triggered and becomes reactive, it is likely that their behavior is a response to their own dysregulated emotion and thought, rather than responding to the incident that actually happened. Once they become anxious or disoriented, a child will continue to loop from the feeling to behaving in a way that locks in the behavior pattern so that nothing new can get in. You've seen a child who becomes so fixed in their response that they cannot hear a word you're saying. That is literally what is happening. It is as if a wall goes up between the child's thinking and their emotion, and nothing you say will help because your words are not even being heard. Breaking this cycle and shifting their behavior requires new sensory inputs and a re-setting of the cycle.

Sensory Response	Intellectual Response	Emotional Response	Behavioral Response
Sense	Think	Feel	Act / Do

Copyright © D. Lambrecht

When a child is dysregulated or disoriented, it is our job to re-orient them, which can only be done through a sensory experience. If you've ever been lost in the woods, or even in a shopping mall, what do you do? You stop, look around, and maybe check a map to re-orient yourself before moving forward. During that moment when you feel lost or disoriented, you will immediately resort back to your senses for the baseline information you need. We must help children with a grounding sensory experience that helps to re-orient them.

Developing the ability to accurately sense, think, feel, and then respond to a situation is part of the maturation process. As it happens, however, the brain does not develop in this linear, logical sequence! The metacognitive skills, or the ability to think about your own thinking, develop at a rudimentary level around age two or three. A deeper capacity to have objectivity and to reflect on thoughts occurs at about age nine, and continues to advance in complexity throughout childhood.

Teaching through the senses is a way of matching the teaching with natural brain development and the developmental stages of childhood.

Stages of Child Development

Children experience the world through their senses, growing from a very physical and sensory understanding into the ability to make cognitive interpretations on what they sense. These interpretations are at first very concrete and literal. Only at the age of eleven or twelve do children begin to develop the ability to reason and think abstractly.

0 to 2 years

The infant/toddler is one giant sense organ with developing sensory-motor systems that allow for a basic understanding of sensory input. Notice that babies will put everything in their mouth, or move toward something with their face first, mouth open and fingers spread wide, in order to take in the sensory information.

When holding an infant, we are always reminded to support their head. Infants have a number of primitive reflexes such as the sucking reflex, grasping reflex, and Moro reflex. These automatic reactions to stimuli allow infants to respond to their environment before any learning has taken place. The Moro reflex or the startle reflex is a response to a sudden loss of support, when the infant feels as if they are falling. When this reflex is activated, babies need to feel enough support to experience their physical edges which helps to soothe their senses. That's why babies respond so well to being wrapped snugly in a blanket, or swaddled. When babies are startled, this activation of the reflex, followed by a calming response is what supports healthy reflex development.

2 - 6 years

This age is the pre-operational stage, where children cannot yet think about their thinking. At this age, children are learning cause and effect, learning to interpret sensory experiences, and even learning to read and write, yet their thinking is still at a more concrete level. In this pre-operational stage, children use symbols to represent their world as evidenced by their pretend play; when a broom becomes a horse, or a tree branch, a magic sword. These symbol images become the building blocks of all learning, from academic to social-emotional learning.

7 - 11 years

This is the concrete-operations stage where children want to know how things operate, how things work. This stage marks the beginning of logical and operational thought, whereby children can begin to work things out internally in their head, using logical thinking. Theory of mind – which is the ability to understand that other people have different perspectives, thoughts, and feelings – develops in this stage. A child's social-cognitive abilities are the cornerstone for developing compassion and healthy social relationships.

12 years

Around age twelve, children have access to abstract thinking abilities, which continue to develop through adulthood. At this stage, children develop reasoning skills – the ability to think about abstract concepts and to think logically to test hypotheses. As children develop greater understanding of their own thought processes, they develop what is known as metacognition, or the ability to think about their thoughts as well as the ideas of others. Early adolescence can be a tumultuous time in a child's development, when there are intense hormonal changes happening in the body, when the mind takes on new capacities, and when social relationships are ever more complex. This new metacognitive capacity supports the maturation process: socially, emotionally, and intellectually.

These widely accepted stages of development were first presented by biologist and psychologist Jean Piaget.

Sociocultural Perspective

Another researcher and psychologist, Lev Vygotsky, expands on Piaget's stages of child development by including a sociocultural perspective such as how the rules of social groups directly influence a person's actions. Often the rules and norms within social groups are unwritten and need to be figured out through observation, testing out new behaviors, and exploring relationships.

School is typically a child's first independent social group with expectations, norms, and standards for behavior. School is where children will be influenced by cultural norms such as "Will adults intervene if I'm feeling picked on?" or "Am I really expected to finish my work?" and "Are children respected?"

School is also where children's existing attitudes and behaviors are reinforced, and new behaviors cultivated. Does the school culture support and develop an attitude of respect and inclusion? Is the school culture focused on producing competitive test scores, no matter the cost to children? Children will either fall in line with the social school culture of the school or rebel against it. Schools, therefore, hold significant sway over a child's development.

Three Foundational Principles

Caulbridge brings together the latest in neuroscience and brain research with a deep understanding of how children learn and grow, balancing current research with collective wisdom. In developing Caulbridge education, we deeply examined both learning and childhood, then landed on these Three Foundational Principles:

1. Childhood is a distinct time.

Childhood is a distinct and valid time in and of itself, and not something to hurry through in a race toward adulthood. Children are not miniature adults – a second-grader is not a deficient twelfth-grader. Children have a unique set of needs that must be met at each developmental stage to progress toward healthy growth and maturity. Only when children are engaged with relevant and developmentally appropriate activities can developmental milestones be reached and real learning occur.

Traditional schools will decide what they want a twelfth grader to know by graduation – then divide that by twelve! This practice is not only ineffective, it is harmful to the young child. As the intensity of information and expectations increase every year for a high school graduate, those expectations are pushed down to the earlier grades, creating developmentally inappropriate standards.

Instead, Caulbridge asks, What is needed for the healthy development of a five-year-old, a seven-year-old, or a ten-year-old, to ensure that grade-level expectations will be met as the child moves through the grades?

Caulbridge correlates educational methods and practices to the developmental changes occurring in the child, and resists the trend to introduce activities or concepts before a child is ready. "The right activity at the right time" is fundamental to a child's learning and development. The kindergartener has substantively different needs and learning capacities than a teenager. When learning reflects the developmental stages of the child, mastery is more likely to be effective, empowering, and enjoyable.

2. Learning is the foundation for a human being to act and behave in new ways.

While information alone can be valuable, learning develops a capacity to translate information into knowledge, knowledge into understanding, understanding into wisdom, and any of these into action. At the same time, acting or behaving in new ways can support healthy brain development and influence learning.

There are two ways in which connections are a part of learning. First, learning has to be connected to something you already know. Recall a time when someone was explaining something and you looked confused, not quite understanding. They might say, "You know, it's like when you...." You immediately reply, "Oh, I get it!"

Second, learning is related to the human connection. In spite of the abundance of online-learning games and software for even the youngest of children, learning requires the context provided by the human interaction for understanding and retention.

A synthesis of Public/Private Venture's research on fostering resilience in children tells us that the most significant indicator of a child's success is the presence of a caring adult – and that children engaged in positive adult relationships are less likely to become involved in negative peer behaviors. Caulbridge educators work to deeply understand each child, and deliver lessons that take them to the next step of their academic and social development. Without knowing why, children respond to this enthusiasm and attention by reflecting back their best achievements. The opposite is also true: children don't learn from people who don't care.

3. Learning is physiological and begins in the body.

Children process, integrate, and act upon information with their entire bodies. Sensory-motor skills, body awareness, maturing reflexes, spatial perception, and focused attention are directly related to a child's capacity for learning.

No part of the central nervous system works alone. Touch aids vision, vision aids balance, balance aids body awareness, body awareness aids movement, and movement aids learning.

— *Carol Kranowitz, Sensory Integration expert*

Movement or body awareness (proprioceptive sense) along with the sense of balance and sense of touch, are foundational to one's ability to perceive and learn. With the healthy development of these sensory-motor functions, brain activity is freed up to develop the more complex, social, and higher-thinking capacities. Perception is the registering of sensory information in the brain. Cognition is the interpretation and understanding of that information. These cognitive, intellectual abilities are higher-level senses that are the last to develop in the human brain. Because the young child's brain is malleable, it is possible to strengthen these foundational aspects of physiological development as a natural process in the learning environment.

Animal Tracking as Literacy!

Observation skills are at the core of problem solving, in that one must first identify the problem and all its components before finding solutions that make the most sense. This skill transfers over to a student's ability to read a situation, notice both the obvious and the more subtle signs, and then develop conclusions based on those observations.

Critical thinking begins with focused attention. Social skills require the ability to read the cues in people's faces and behaviors. Problem solving begins with the ability to observe a situation and possible solutions. All these skills are inherent in animal tracking and wilderness outings.

Every parent wants their child to be able to walk into a situation, assess what is happening, and then be able to act accordingly. Initially I thought that our monthly Wilderness Day was a wonderful experience for the children, one where they could learn primitive skills and gain confidence in nature. It turned out to be so much more. Soon, we began to see the effects of students' new animal tracking and observation skills in the classroom.

Tracking is the science and art of observing animal footprints and other signs for the purpose of gaining understanding of the landscape, along with the systems that make up the environment. The skilled tracker is able to observe their surroundings, discern clues, re-create some details, and make predictions about what might have happened. When students come upon an animal track, they first find twigs to frame the specimen, marking it for observation and study. Then the investigations, inquiries and wonderings begin. Is this a deer? Which direction is it traveling? Is it walking alone or are there others? Is this a mama deer or baby? Was she going to find water? Where would she go for water and what would she eat? Kindergarten students may have ideas or stories about the mama and baby deer, while questions from the older grades may span out to take in the time of day, the weather conditions, the flora and fauna of the area, the watershed, and so on.

On a recent Wilderness Day, trekking through a dry creek bed, our students came upon fallen trees that created a natural dam in the riverbed where they discovered a ball heaven! The dam was filled with worn and dirty basketballs, soccer balls, kickballs, and tennis balls. The children decided this must be the place where old balls go when they die. An obvious first assumption – yet with a bit of guided inquiry, they concluded that there must be a park or schoolyard upstream, and especially with last year's record rains, the balls were lost to the rushing waters.

Practical Arts and Skills

Why do we teach practical arts and skills?

We teach fire building not because we expect that our students will be stranded in the wilderness and need to survive; rather, for the sense of accomplishment, confidence, and mastery it provides. Armed with a new skill, and sometimes one they can teach their parents, a child experiences their enthusiasm for learning come alive.

Activities such as carving, knitting, cooking, and building are essential to encourage children to work with their hands to create something practical. Working with the hands in rhythmical movements promotes the mental operations of logic, reaching conclusions, forming judgments, and comprehension.

Working with the hands also calms the nervous system and further develops intelligence, which is formed through activity, movement, and manual dexterity.

Practical arts also have a way of strengthening the inner initiative by bringing a warming balance to a child's physical and cognitive expression. Our physics curriculum teaches us that everything is propelled by warmth: gasoline/combustion fuels our cars, the sun fuels the plants, and healthy food fuels our bodies. Intellect and thinking forces are cooling in nature. Pure intellectual thinking may bring about ideas or solutions that, without the warmth of the human heart, may not really work for humanity.

Integrating visual and practical arts throughout the day can help to open a child's mind and heart in a balanced way. Making something beautiful helps children cultivate a deeper respect for both their own creations and the works of others.

IN THE CLASSROOM

Beginning with finger-knitting in kindergarten, children can quickly produce beautiful bracelets or knitted chains. Children who were once fidgeting in circle time are now able to sit and focus on their knitting, and feel accomplished with their masterpiece. In first grade, when children progress to knitting needles, we see their attention span go from five or six minutes to fifteen or twenty minutes – almost overnight. The small motor development and hand/eye coordination it takes for knitting supports a child's ability to focus.

No Child Left Inside: Connecting Children, Nature, and Learning

As an educator, I know that this forty-five-minute trip to the creek to observe, catch, and then graph the life cycle of frogs is more than a fun outing. I see a lesson that incorporates all the benefits of nature with developmental movement, positive social dynamics, and relevant content. I see a student – who took on a task so momentous that it required a complete change of clothing – emerge triumphant. The confidence of such an outing translates to the courage necessary to take on new learning in the classroom. The physical exertion and time in nature help to calm the nervous system and focus the mind – which is required for the math lesson later in the day.

In his recent best-selling book, *Last Child in The Woods*, Richard Louv points to the increasing alienation between children and nature as a contributor of childhood anxiety, attention-deficit disorders, and developmental delays in our children. Louv defines this condition as Nature-Deficit Disorder.

Caulbridge understands that learning is a natural process when you integrate nature, arts, movement, friendship, and academics.

Practices and Habits

Caulbridge education fosters strong habits and practices in children. It was the great sage, Bruce Lee, who said, "Under duress, we don't rise to the level of our expectations, we fall to the level of our practice."

We want children to have strong habits of mind and heart. Learning fractions requires the same practiced habits as learning compassion.

Scientists studied the brain activity of high school students while computing calculus problems. As the brain accesses basic, concrete math facts, the mid-section of the brain lights up in the MRI. When the student switches to the calculus problem, needing higher-level thinking, the frontal cortex lights up. It was obvious by looking at the MRI when students had to go back and search for information not readily available. Most students who had to go back to retrieve basic math facts couldn't hold their mental picture of the problem, and were unable to track the advanced reasoning and thinking needed to solve calculus equations.

Working memory has been compared to the desktop on your computer: a place to sort, edit or produce work that will be stored for later retrieval. Children process information cognitively using their working memory, to be stored later in the long-term-memory part of the brain. Almost all information stored in our working memory and not rehearsed or practiced is lost within thirty seconds! The capacity of working memory is limited to only a very small number of elements: as many as seven, or as few as four, depending on the complexity of the elements.

Practice is the only way to move information from our working memory to either our long-term, semantic memory, which is the memory of knowledge and facts; or to our procedural memory, which allows us to perform a task automatically, like riding a bike.

Caulbridge intentionally builds strong practices that develop the neural pathways for a child to move between the ability to understand and process information and the ability to store and retrieve information at will. Building strong practices will support more than academic success: it also develops confidence, resourcefulness, initiative, capabilities, and agency in children.

IN THE CLASSROOM

I stepped in at the end of the day when a teacher had to leave early. The class was running late and the students were lining up at the door for dismissal. When the teacher saw me, she indicated that I might walk those who are ready outside to meet parents for pick-up. Waiting at the front of the line was Emma, who calmly said, "No, I'm going to wait here where we always line up until everybody is ready." She was respecting the daily routine, and I joined her in the practiced habit of waiting patiently to be dismissed.

"We don't practice until we get it right; we practice until we can't get it wrong."

— *Geno Auriemma*

Why Teaching Academics by Skill Level vs. Grade Level Is Better for Your Child

Grouping students by skill level rather than grade level for math and language arts meets the needs of those students who are ready for more-advanced academics, as well as those who are struggling and need to catch up. At Caulbridge School, students across the grades move among these skill-level groups, depending on what skills they need practice to master.

For a student who struggles, it does not mean that they'll always be below grade level. Once the foundational reading skills and basic math facts are solid, children might progress quite quickly. It is impossible however, for children to learn third-grade math when they have not mastered the basic first- or second-grade level expectations. Our approach to remediation is different than sending your third-grader to the first-grade classroom for math lessons! Because all students are grouped by skill level, there is no grade-level distinction for children to compare to or compete against. If the goal is strong academic skills, it is necessary to create an environment that supports optimal learning, using structured academics and sequential mastery of skills.

This model also supports children who are advanced beyond the kindergarten-level expectations of basic letters and numbers, and can move on to more-structured academics that build upon their solid one-to-one correspondence and letter/sound recognition.

If a kindergarten student is reading at second-grade level, isn't it better to move them up to first grade so they won't be bored? No. And here's why.

We have seen that a five-year-old who is an advanced reader is NOT a young first-grader; he is a really intelligent kindergartener. This means that developmentally, he is best supported by the routines and practices of the kindergarten classroom: learning to be a student, building his stamina and body/brain connection, and developing the output level needed for the grades. A really smart kindergarten child will demonstrate cognitive capacities beyond their years. While they are ready for the input of more intellectual stimulation, they may not be ready for the work output required of a first-grader. A younger child's sensory-motor, sensory-processing, spatial-awareness, and social skills are still developing and will not support the added workload to their body and brain. Moving ahead prematurely will result in frustration and breakdowns in the emotional, social, physical, and academic areas of a child's life.

Our model of teaching also solves some of the issues for children with summer birthdays. When my daughter turned six in early summer, I was faced with the dilemma of putting her in first grade, or into another year of kindergarten. Trying to sort out this decision, I commented to her teacher that in some ways she's ready for first grade. Her teacher agreed, and added that in some ways she's ready for third grade! But, at what cost? Looking back, the decision to give her another year of kindergarten was the best one at the time. It would have been even better with the option of fostering her academic development in a way that matched her capabilities.

Caulbridge Teaches Oracy

Oracy includes speaking and listening skills, rhetorical techniques, self-regulation, and presence. Can a student look you in the eye, listen to another's perspective, and offer a reasoned point of view?

Oracy supports numeracy and literacy skills for a more balanced and relevant education.

Numeracy is the ability to understand and work with numbers.

Literacy is the ability to read, write, and draw knowledge from information.

Oracy adds capabilities and confidence in communications and relationships. Self-expression, reading an audience, building on the views of others, and well-developed ideas are important life skills.

We are preparing children for a time of new paradigms, for jobs that have not yet been created, for unknown challenges, and for undiscovered solutions. Our world needs adaptive thinkers with strength of heart and character.

Caulbridge educators want students to have the mindset, skillset, and internal architecture to navigate their world. In addition to the academics, arts, and self-efficacy skills, we teach communication and relationship skills necessary for our students to confidently engage with the world.

We teach oracy skills that are age appropriate and that correlate with the child's physiological, intellectual, and social-emotional development.

In first grade, students practice listening, taking turns, eye contact, and recitation. Lessons that support sensory-motor skills and spatial awareness help develop the confidence and presence necessary for effective communication.

Building upon these practices, students are provided opportunities to develop linguistics, verbal and non-verbal communication, and critical-thinking skills. By eighth grade, students will be able to critically examine ideas and opinions, then develop and deliver a reasoned point of view.

Social-Emotional Learning

Schools often use social-emotional curriculum activities to help students name their emotions, in hopes they will be able to manage those emotions. A child's ability to name feelings is not the same as emotional development, any more than our ability to identify healthy foods is the same as being healthy!

As a school leader, my email is filled with advertising and promotions for the latest curriculum and school-program services. Recently I received a pitch for a program that made my heart ache. It was a program claiming that teaching anger management during preschool will lay the foundation for school readiness. Suggesting that by proactively teaching emotion identification, children will learn to self-regulate and be successful in kindergarten. That's impossible. Preschool children do not have the self-reflection and discernment skills needed to self-regulate when they are emotionally triggered.

Children's social skills develop best with consistent, age-appropriate expectations that can be practiced in a supportive way whenever it is needed. Role playing in class is generally less effective for actual social development, since the young child is not readily able to step into another's shoes or take another's perspective. Instead, children are more likely to learn social skills during imaginative, free-play time. Skills to resolve social conflicts are best practiced in real-time, concrete interactions guided by a nurturing adult.

Children learn, explore, and struggle together as part of their natural and healthy development. Conflict between students is a natural and necessary part of learning. Children learn to engage in relationships with others – and learn to know themselves – through friendships and cooperation, as well as through competition and challenges.

Conflict is not the same as bullying. Conflict may happen when, for example, students disagree on the rules of a game at recess. This kind of conflict can be sorted out by changing the game or redirecting the children to join a different game with other students or having some alone time. Bullying, on the other hand, happens when one child attempts to dominate another child or the entire situation.

Bullying is distinctly different from regular conflict – and it cannot be tolerated. Bullying is generally repeated behavior that is planned and/ or done on purpose. Bullying includes a discrepancy in power within the relationship, where someone is trying to gain control over another person while simultaneously blaming the other child for the bullying behavior.

Caulbridge educators assume the duty to manage conflict in a manner most supportive of all involved. Keeping a watchful eye, sometimes faculty will allow the children to work through their conflicts independently to best support learning and growth. Faculty may also use the children's conflict as an opportunity for the explicit teaching of new skills, behaviors, empathy, and compassion.

Conflict is a normal part of childhood, which actually helps develop important personal and relationship skills. Learning to handle conflict, however, can only happen in a safe social environment, where there is respect, empathy, and fairness. Children can learn from conflict only when guided by adults who know how to set up a safe environment, remain calm, and focus on the best outcomes for children.

As I approached a small group of nine-year-old girls, a mother was asking her daughter to apologize to the others, and asking the others to acknowledge the apology with what they thought might have been their part in the disagreement. The girls initially seemed surprised at the request, since it was Monday morning at school and the disagreement happened last week. However, the girls obliged, and went skipping on to class. Then the mother turned to me, visibly anxious, and said, "I just want them to really get it this time so it doesn't happen again."

She was hoping that her nine-year-old daughter would never have another disagreement, social conflict or difficult relationship. First of all, any nine-year-old has plenty of social conflict yet to come, and second, the conflicts among friends are a necessary part of developing conflict resolution, social skills, and learning to be in relationships.

While the mother's goal for her daughter – to have healthy friendships and speak up for herself – is shared by most parents, the idea that children can skip over the childhood social development and go right to assertive communication and healthy boundaries is unrealistic. This lofty expectation becomes a setup for children who do not have the maturity to relate in this way. It also become a sticking point for parents who might view a child's behavior as something they should know by now, rather than something the child is still practicing.

Social-emotional development goes hand in hand with academic development. Children do not learn when they are socially or emotionally anxious, fearful, or dysregulated. Being confident in their own social skills allows a student to engage in class.

IN THE CLASSROOM

Joey avoided conflict whenever possible. By age nine, he'd seen enough unresolved conflict and blame to believe that he's better off keeping to himself. He seemed happy playing by himself, and didn't take much notice of the social scene around him. Spending time alone is fine, but it had progressed to the point that he was unable to ask for help. Joey was struggling in the classroom, and didn't have much interest in learning.

Joey's underdeveloped spatial awareness made it difficult to "find his place" with his peers. Isolating himself did not allow for practicing social skills. Using collaborative games and movement activities, our teachers worked to improve his spatial awareness.

After a few weeks of the games and activities, Joey ran to a teacher and asked for help. He teared up and said, "Grayson is digging too close to my hole. Can you help me tell him that I don't like that?" This was the first time Joey demonstrated his ability to negotiate conflict at school. Now we often hear him express, "I don't like that, what about this?"

His improved spatial awareness helped him to be more confident in his environment, with his peer interactions, and in the classroom.

When Sarah came to Caulbridge in the first grade, she had mature social skills, often relying on manipulation to sustain her social interactions. Her peers often needed a break from her bossy behaviors. When left alone, Sarah would try to find someone else to coax into her games. Her peers quickly caught on to these behaviors and began to stand up for their own ideas and needs.

Unchecked, this behavior could easily accelerate to the point of bullying, but this was a case of learned and practiced behavior. At home, Sarah was accustomed to spending most of her time around her younger siblings, where she was naturally more capable and took charge of the play.

Explicit teaching of social skills helped her notice that her behavior was not getting the results she wanted, and to realize she could be a better friend. She slowly learned to release control, eventually asking what her peers wanted to play, and willingly joining games where she had to follow their rules.

SECTION 6
More on Caulbridge

How Caulbridge Compares – Teaching/Learning Matrix

Education has become profoundly influenced by textbook, testing, and technology companies that dictate the teaching and learning: a case of the tail wagging the dog.

Using Teaching/Learning as the x/y axis, I developed this matrix to answer the question: How does Caulbridge compare? Starting with our Three Foundational Principles, Caulbridge education weaves together the best evidence-based practices that have stood the test of time, with innovative approaches appropriate for children now and in their evolving future.

TEACHING/LEARNING MATRIX

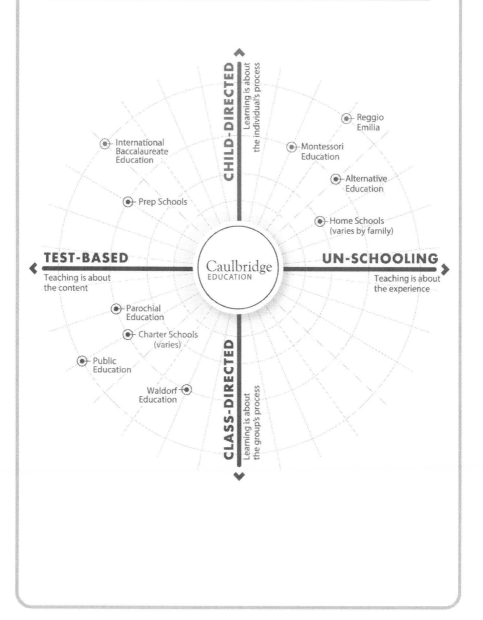

CHILD-DIRECTED — Learning is about the individual's process

CLASS-DIRECTED — Learning is about the group's process

TEST-BASED — Teaching is about the content

UN-SCHOOLING — Teaching is about the experience

Caulbridge EDUCATION

- Reggio Emilia
- International Baccalaureate Education
- Montessori Education
- Alternative Education
- Prep Schools
- Home Schools (varies by family)
- Parochial Education
- Charter Schools (varies)
- Public Education
- Waldorf Education

TEACHING CONTINUUM

TEST-BASED ‹········ **DEVELOPMENTALLY APPROPRIATE** ·······› **UN-SCHOOLING**

⚠ RISKS
Standards and curriculum may not be developmentally appropriate.

CAULBRIDGE
aligns curriculum methods and activities to the cognitive, social/emotional and physical stages of the developing child.

⚠ RISKS
May miss opportunities that support healthy development.

⊘ BENEFITS
Consistency in education and metrics to measure progress.

⊘ BENEFITS
Promotes individual freedom and potential creativity

LEARNING CONTINUUM

CLASS-DIRECTED ‹···· **CHILD-FOCUSED** ····› **CHILD-DIRECTED**

⚠ RISKS
Child may become unbalanced if one capacity is developed at expense of others.

CAULBRIDGE
places the child at the center, using an education team that considers activities and support related the child's development.

⚠ RISKS
Child may not be noticed or challenged academically or socially.

⊘ BENEFITS
Autonomy, self-reliance and individual learning style developed.

⊘ BENEFITS
Social and collaboration skills are practiced.

On one side of the Teaching Continuum (horizontal axis) is a Test-Based approach where *Teaching Is About the Content*. This is often referred to as "teaching to the test," or "teach it/test it." It is quite typical in traditional public schools. The potential benefit with this approach is a consistent set of grade-level curriculum standards and metrics to measure student progress.

Where this approach falls short is in the assumptions that all children learn at the same rate or process learning in the same way. Another risk is that these content standards are generated from a top-down model and often are not developmentally appropriate for the younger child.

The opposite end of the "Teaching" continuum is some form of "un-schooling," where *Teaching is About the Experience*. This is based on the belief that everything a child needs to learn can come from real-world experiences. While it is true that children can gain practical knowledge and skills from experiences, it is more likely that a child may have an interesting experience, but it will depend completely on the skill of the facilitator to determine if learning is happening. A benefit associated with this approach is that it may promote individual creativity and freedom for some children. A risk, however, would be missing the opportunity for coherent learning or healthy child development.

The Learning Continuum (vertical axis) ranges from a class-directed approach where *Learning is About the Group's Process*, meaning the class moves ahead together and no one moves until everyone is ready. The priority is on the collective and social learning of the class. A likely risk of this approach is that individual children may not be noticed, or challenged academically or socially. A potential benefit of this approach is that social and collaboration skills are being practiced.

At the top of the Learning Continuum is a child-directed approach where *Learning is About the Individual's Process*, which represents independent study or self-paced learning. A potential risk of this approach is that one aspect of a child's learning or development is accelerated at the expense of other capacities. On the other hand, developing a child's autonomy, self-reliance, and individual learning style may be a beneficial result of this approach.

In developing Caulbridge education, we reviewed and intentionally selected the best evidence-based practices, and aligned those practices with the stages of the developing child.

Anyone who has worked in the education field for more than five years has seen curriculum and teaching trends come and go, then come back again under a different name! Teachers usually pick and choose curriculum and teaching practices based on their own personal preference, and will often boast of blending a little of this and a little of that to make an interesting curriculum. The problem with blending pieces from varying curricula is that it dilutes the effectiveness of the results, much like blending your beautiful water color paints until you end up with an ugly brown mess. When selecting curriculum and teaching methods, it is essential to maintain the fidelity of the method to ensure the results. Caulbridge has very intentionally selected its curriculum, teaching methods, and school practices so as to support the developing child.

Formative and Summative Assessments

Like the traditional public schools, we adopt consistent grade-level expectations to help assess a child's progress in learning. In place of the standardized tests, however, Caulbridge uses both formative and summative assessments. Formative assessments help teachers identify concepts, learning outcomes, or skills that students are struggling to understand, for the purpose of improving upon instruction and student learning *while it's happening*. Summative assessments are used to evaluate student learning progress and achievement at the conclusion of a thematic unit, or at regular intervals of time throughout the school year.

Evidence of Learning

- Evidence of a student's learning is demonstrated through the work that students produce, as well as their participation in activities. Using a lesson book or portfolio, students essentially create their own textbook, which includes essays, drawings, maps, poetry, or descriptions of lab experiments.

- Caulbridge educators regularly assess students in math, language arts, and all course curricula, as well as oracy, sensory-motor, executive-functioning and social-emotional skills.

The Public or Private-School Dilemma

Young parents generally see themselves as either a public-school family or private-school family, a preference often based on their own school experience. Self-proclaimed private-school families sometimes choose a school based on family loyalties, location, or extra-curricular activities, or they may shop for a school that reflects their family's priorities and values.

Families who assumed they would attend the neighborhood public school are often unsettled as they find themselves considering private school. It's only after realizing their child is not a good candidate for the traditional public school that they begin their search.

I always recommend that parents begin their search by discovering what approach and environment will support their child's success. If a public school is the right fit, then free is better. If it is not the right fit, then free is too high a price. When children struggle early on in school, those struggles almost always escalate until it affects not only the student's learning, but also their self-concept and behaviors. The added financial considerations of a private school can be a stretch for many families, but when it comes to our children, that *no-matter-what-it-takes* gene seems to kick in.

Waldorf or Montessori

When considering Waldorf or Montessori, many parents assume that the two are similar in their educational approach. While both philosophies include the use of natural materials and emphasize practical life activities, philosophically, they are quite opposite.

Waldorf education is a class-directed approach, holding all students to the expectations of the class as a whole, and only progressing when the entire class is ready to move on. This reflects an understanding of developing a child's success through conformity to the social relationships and readiness of the class.

Montessori is in the opposite quadrant from Waldorf, using the child's interest as the guiding factor in deciding the curriculum. Montessori uses a more individualized approach, where children set the pace and direction of their learning.

Reggio Emilia

Reggio Emilia education is a project-based, free-form approach to children learning about what they are interested in as a group. This is based in a constructivist model, which believes that if children are engaged with something they are interested in, they will learn. Reggio Emilia also reflects a priority on the children rather than on the teaching.

Alternative Schools

Progressive or Alternative schools are often started by parent initiatives with strong ideas about what kind of school experience they want for their children. Frustrated when they cannot find a school that matches their vision, they often gather around the kitchen table and work to launch their new private school. These schools are usually run by parents who are involved with all the processes from sitting on school boards, overseeing school governance, and even hiring teachers. When parents are not professional educators, they may prioritize their own children's experience, even at the expense of sound educational practices. Without strong leadership and a system of accountability to maintain the quality of the educational outcomes, schools can be vulnerable to a parent who learns of a trendy new program or idea and wants to bring it to the teachers to implement because they want their own children to experience it. When schools are dependent upon financial contributions from these parents, it can be easy to veer away from recognized best practices in education.

The Caulbridge Difference

Caulbridge education provides a healthy sensory experience for children through nature and natural products and supplies made of high-quality materials. In these ways, Caulbridge classrooms and campuses may reflect the environment of Montessori or Waldorf schools. Where we distinguish ourselves is in the curriculum: bringing structured academics, explicit teaching, differentiated learning, and a broad world view into the learning environment. Caulbridge has a primary teacher for each grade level, and a team of teachers who have all had the same training to support specific subject areas. Waldorf schools are teacher-centric, and teachers stay with the class through the grades. Similarly, Montessori students remain with the same teacher for three-year cycles.

In contrast to Montessori's child-directed education, Caulbridge uses the child's interest as a doorway into the lesson rather than using the child's interest to drive the curriculum. While a nine-year-old can let you know what they are interested in, they are certainly not qualified to determine what's in their best interest.

As in Reggio Emilia education, Caulbridge agrees that the most important people in the classroom are the children; however, Caulbridge understands it is the teachers who create student engagement through well-prepared classrooms and explicit teaching of lessons. We understand that the quality of the learning is the job of the teachers, rather than the students.

Caulbridge schools are run by experienced educators, holding to a quality teaching, learning, and school experience that parents can trust. Parents at Caulbridge are warmly invited into the community and conversation – not, however, into the curriculum – which helps protect enrolled families from unexpected drifts in educational philosophy.

A Day in the Life of Your Caulbridge Student

The daily class schedule is designed around the needs of children, in support of optimal learning and healthy development. Longer class periods allow for varied activities in approaching the subject content, and fewer transitions for children within the day. Students are welcomed into the classroom for their morning greeting, then they head outdoors for their circle activities to wake up their senses in preparation for optimal learning. The remainder of the day is broken into three main components:

Thematic Units

- Academic content and context are taught in thematic units of two to six weeks of focused study.
- Everything the child is learning has a relationship to a developmentally appropriate and academically relevant thematic unit.

Skill Building

- Daily Math and Language Arts practice builds strong skills, habits, and routines.
- PE / Movement / Games
- Music: singing, percussion, recorder, and ensemble instruments.

Experiential Learning — Practical Application

- Arts and sciences that are integrated and experiential serve to open a child's heart and mind in a balanced way.

- Practical Arts include handwork, gardening, building, sewing, and cooking.

- Fine Arts include drawing, painting, clay modeling, music, and drama.

- Environmental Sciences include Earth Studies, water cycles, ecology, and plant and animal life

- Chores at the end of the day help nurture executive-function skills and encourage students to care for their school.

The Morning Lesson delivers the main curriculum content and concepts in an extended class period. The lessons are taught in a multi-disciplinary, multi-sensory, experiential way without standard textbooks. Instead, the children make their own portfolio which includes essays, drawings, maps, poetry, or descriptions of lab experiments. Teachers work to create lessons and classroom activities that are responsive to a variety of student readiness levels, learning styles, and individual capacities. Students create their own lesson books or portfolios of work. In addition to our specific curriculum materials, teachers assemble a collection of resources to integrate the artistic and experiential components within the academics. Because we teach in thematic units, integrating the curriculum, we find that standard textbooks lack the inter-connectedness of subject content.

Math and Language Arts is taught by skill level rather than grade level. Students are grouped by the concepts and skills they need to learn. Daily practice builds strong numeracy and literacy skills and learning habits.

Differentiated lessons can address each child's learning style and abilities. Though the class is all working on the same topic, the expectations for practice time may vary to best build on a student's abilities.

Caulbridge Teachers

When a woman heard we were hiring teachers, she exclaimed, "I know an amazing teacher, my daughter had her in third grade." When I asked what made her such an amazing teacher, this mother replied, "Well, she just LOVED my daughter!"

Let's start there. When teachers work to develop a meaningful, respectful relationship, children can learn to trust the authority of an adult which later is the basis for developing their own inner authority and competencies. When teachers hold and project a steady picture of the child's best self, children rise up to meet those expectations and strive to reflect back the best version of themselves.

Caulbridge educators work from a child-development perspective and understand that meeting the child's needs relevant to their phase of development is foundational to learning and school success. All behavior reflects a child's skills, limitations, emotions, and moods within any given environment. It is the educator's job to interpret the behavior and either reinforce or shift behaviors toward healthy development.

Teachers create a calm and inviting environment that holds space for relationships and learning. Clear expectations and boundaries held by nurturing adults will help to shift a child's behavior away from habits and behaviors that may not serve them.

Caulbridge educators use rich language to deliver the curriculum lessons and clear language to hold boundaries and student expectations. Teachers work with an open heart and consistent patience. Children respond best in situations they can trust, and will often shut down or act out if they sense an environment where there is an air of disrespect, inconsistencies, harshness or intolerance.

The young child learns through imitation, which means all Caulbridge educators must be worthy of imitation.

SECTION 7

About Us

Why Parents Love Caulbridge

"We moved to Marin so my son could attend this school, and it was completely worth it! When your child is happy and thriving, the family life is more harmonious and life as a parent just works better. It will be great to have our daughter start kindergarten in the fall as well." – *Parent*

"I have high hopes for my son and wanted to be sure his talents were recognized and fostered. We want him to use his strong intellect, to have good friends, and to be a happy person in the world. We looked everywhere. I'm convinced that Caulbridge educators understand my son. They see his strengths and his challenges. Just as important, the team is very responsive to my questions and I often seek their guidance on the best way to support my son." – *Parent*

"I knew, after the first day at Caulbridge, that it was the right school for him. Our five-year-old never wanted to go to kindergarten. He hated school. After just one day, he asked me if he could go back to Caulbridge the next day. It just got better and better after that. Instead of a child who came home from school unregulated and unfocused, I now had a child who came home completely calm, happy, and eager to keep learning.

"We are so grateful for this school's common sense approach to learning, where kids have movement breaks and access to nature, and each child's interests and abilities can be fully realized. Thank you, Caulbridge!" – *Parent*

"Our son has been thriving with the smaller class size and more individualized attention, as well as the focus on daily physical activity and outdoor time for learning and playing. And, despite the smaller class size, the socialization aspects of school are continually practiced and developed at Caulbridge School because of the group learning and activities. The small class size also allows the amazing Ms. Rachel to figure out how each of her students learns, and to tailor her teaching to each child's learning style. For example, she quickly realized that our son easily memorizes sentences and book passages, and she devised fun ways of ensuring that he is actually reading – as opposed to reciting what he has memorized." – *Parent*

"As business owners ourselves, we were attracted to the idea of a school that has combined the best of the other education models and created what I have affectionately told others "is the school you would create if you were building your own school." The school may be new, but the professionals involved bring many years of experience – in addition to a genuine passion for their work, and a nurturing attitude toward the students. We are seeing first-hand that a happy child is a more eager learner, and we are all happy with our decision to switch to Caulbridge School." – *Parent*

"Yesterday my child asked to be excused from the table – I was shocked!" – *Parent*

About the Author

Debra Lambrecht
Founder, Caulbridge Education

Since 1981, Ms. Lambrecht has worked with schools and youth leaders to influence positive change in the way we meet the needs of children. Debra has provided professional development training, along with strategic and organizational consulting for hundreds of schools and youth organizations across the country; and has served as School Director of a private preschool through 8th grade. As founder of Caring About Kids, she created a unique mentor program that was replicated throughout the United States; and authored several youth development publications including training manuals that became required text for CA State University Master's counseling program. Ms. Lambrecht's innovative program models have been recognized as exemplary by United Way, National Public Radio, and Rotary International. Debra has also had the privilege of representing Rotary International while presenting her work at the United Nations International Youth Strategies Summit.

In a culmination of her, work Debra is compelled to redesign an education for our time. "We understand more about brain science and child development than ever before. In spite of the extensive research and experience, our current school system remains locked into an outdated education paradigm."

Caulbridge education began as a desire to step back, and to answer the more fundamental questions: "What is an ideal education for our time, for the children before us today? How can we break the cycle of dysfunction? Could we start with an intention to raise happy, healthy children?" Finding the answer to these questions within current research and collective wisdom, Debra launched a private school in Marin, California as part of a larger social mission to build a network of Caulbridge Schools.

Contact Information

Caulbridge School

San Rafael, California

415-481-1243

https://CaulbridgeSchool.org

admin@caulbridgeschool.org

Made in the USA
Columbia, SC
19 September 2019